Rules of
Engagement

Rules of Engagement

Finding Faith and Purpose in a Disconnected World

CHAD HENNINGS

Unless otherwise indicated, Scriptures are taken from the HOLY BIBLE: NEW INTERNATIONAL VERSION®. Copyright © 1973, 1978, 1984 by International Bible Society. Used by permission of Zondervan Publishing House. All rights reserved.

Scriptures noted KJV are taken from the King James Version of the Bible.

Scriptures noted NASB are taken from the New American Standard Bible®, Copyright © 1960, 1962, 1963, 1968, 1972, 1975, 1977, 1995 by The Lockman Foundation. Used by permission.

Scriptures noted NKJV are taken from the NEW KING JAMES VERSION. Copyright © 1979, 1980, 1982, Thomas Nelson, Inc., Publishers.

Scriptures noted NLT are from the *Holy Bible*, New Living Translation, Copyright © 1996. Used by permission of Tyndale House Publishers, Inc., Wheaton, Illinois 60189. All rights reserved.

www.ChadHennings.com

Library of Congress Cataloging-in-Publication Data

Hennings, Chad.
Rules of engagement : finding faith and purpose in a
disconnected world / Chad Hennings.
p. cm.
ISBN 978-0-9909649-1-9
1. Conduct of life.   2. Christian life.   3. Interpersonal relations—
Religious aspects—Christianity.   I. Title.
BJ1581.2.H4485 2010
248.8'42—dc22
2009027911

CONTENTS

ACKNOWLEDGMENTS

I want to thank God for His grace that saved me, a sinner in the ranks of "the greatest of sinners," as Saint Paul described himself. The whole concept of grace is beyond my understanding: how a sovereign God loved me enough to send His one and only Son to take my place of judgment before Him. It is difficult for my human mind to grasp such love, but I am eternally grateful to Him. That is why I serve such an awesome God. It is not only my duty but my pleasure and passion to join Him in His work.

I also want to thank:

My wife, Tammy. You are the balance to my life. Even though many times we see the situations differently, together we are a powerful combo. God knew what He was doing when He brought you into my life.

My son, Chase. You have shown me more inner strength than any individual I know. You are a true inspiration to me. I am proud to be your father and call you my son.

My daughter, Brenna. You have brought a light into our family. Your passion and faith will move mountains. You are truly my hope.

ACKNOWLEDGMENTS

My parents, Bill and Barb. You modeled for me what it means to live life with purpose and to enjoy the gift of being able to work hard to fulfill my individual, God-given passion.

The rest of my extended family. You all were the first to show me that it takes a *family* to raise a child. Being a part of that team is my legacy.

My head coaches, Reese Morgan, Jerry Eckenrod, and Fisher DeBerry. Thank you for being mentors and leaders of young men.

Jack Deere, Jim Lane, Dudley Hall, and Glenn Terrell. Whether you guys know it or not, you started me down this path of seeking what it means to be part of a group of men standing shoulder to shoulder.

And finally my Wingmen. I wish I could name you all individually, but that is a book in and of itself. You show me every week what it means to be part of the body of Christ. I am grateful to share my life with you.

To Be a Man

Three Super Bowl rings in nine seasons with the Dallas Cowboys.

Air Force fighter pilot with more than forty humanitarian missions to aid the Kurds during the first Gulf War.

Winner of the Outland Trophy as the best interior lineman in the country while playing football at the Air Force Academy.

Husband, father, businessman, motivational speaker for religious and business audiences.

Before all that, Iowa high school state heavyweight wrestling champion.

To the outside observer, I've fulfilled just about every boyhood dream imaginable. But on the inside, for reasons dating back to childhood, I always felt isolated and alone.

Most people picture growing up in small-town America as an extended episode of *Leave It to Beaver*—full of happy-go-lucky buddies and close friendships that last a lifetime. But my strongest memory from childhood is sitting by myself at our family farm, throwing rocks into a nearby creek and crying out to God over the pain of loneliness. It hurt so much, and at the time I felt like there was nothing I could do about it. As a boy, I hid my feelings as best I could, even from my family. I didn't want anyone to know how much I was hurting. In my mind, that would have been embarrassing and totally unacceptable. Showing emotional vulnerability just wasn't something that boys did.

By the time I'd enrolled at the Air Force Academy, things hadn't really changed. I had friends in and out of the Air Force, but in reality, I was pretty much a loner. I played football at the Academy and got along with the guys on the team, but I never opened up and bared my soul to any of them. Even though I had some great friends, there was nothing I would describe like that covenantal relationship between David and Jonathan that the Bible describes. No one knew my deepest, darkest secrets, my hopes, my fears, or my passions. And one of those passions was to play professional football—a dream I'd had ever since I was a kid.

When the Gulf War ended and the Soviet Union collapsed, the Air Force waived all of my commitment time through a "reduction in force" (read: downsizing), along with hundreds of other officers. That meant I could finally pursue my lifelong dream of playing in the NFL. Still, even then it was a struggle for me to leave the Air Force, because I felt like I was stepping out on my commitment to my country. But no one knew about that struggle, because I didn't tell anybody. There was nobody I felt I could tell.

When I tried out for the Cowboys, I was a twenty-six-year-old rookie—four years older than the majority of guys coming out for the team. I could compete with them physically and "hang" with them socially, but I was isolated. Going through that first training camp at St. Edward's in Austin, Texas, was tough. Imagine this—the stress level of changing careers, moving your family from one country to another, starting a job in hundred-degree weather in Austin, and competing at a professional level where you've never competed before, after a four-year layoff. That was my world.

I always tried to be personable, but to let the other players beyond my outer facade as a man—that had to be earned. It happens over time. As a result, during that first training camp when I was striving to make the team, I was missing my family. I was incredibly isolated, and all by choice. I remember sitting in the cinder block dorm with no TV and no radio, just a bed and some books, passing the hours at night or in between practices, just thinking, "God, what have I done? What am I doing here?" On some level, I was still that eleven-year-old boy feeling totally alone.

At the time, the team had only six defensive linemen, so I had to play every down of every preseason game, all the scrimmages, all the practices. It beat me down physically, but the worst thing was that once the regular season started, I never even played in the first seven games of my rookie season. I thought, I'm an abysmal failure.

By my choice, there was still no one to talk to. At home, I had to be the strong one for my family. My wife had followed me all over the world, and now, much of the time, she was left alone. You can probably imagine the stress in our marriage from dealing with that.

It took me more than two years before I really had earned the starting position, so I didn't feel totally comfortable in the NFL for all that time. There was a learning curve or growth process to the idea of accepting my career. I was still isolated emotionally from my teammates, due to my personality—the same as in elementary school. I didn't want to reach out—I didn't know how. I just continued with the superficial friendships I had my whole life. My life was a fabulous success—on the outside. But I was torn up on the inside, physically and emotionally.

From a spiritual perspective, I was a believing Christian, but one who "punched the clock" when it came to faith, not one who relied on God. Church and religion were things I went through because my parents wanted me to do so. I believed that Jesus Christ paid the price for my sins, but there's a difference between believing that superficially versus believing it as if you bet your life on it. I was an outward success—a Super Bowl winner—but my life felt like I was eating nothing but bread for every meal. I was getting filled, even satisfied, but there was no taste. There was a blandness to my life that I didn't like but I couldn't figure out how to change. I remember thinking, there's got to be more to life than this. The outside world looked at me like I was Superman. But instead, I was still failing as a man. I was still trying to go it alone, totally relying on myself in all things instead of seeing myself as a part of a team—God's team.

Then, after four years in the League, something happened that I couldn't fix or overcome. Overnight, my son, Chase, went from a typical, healthy two-year-old to a boy fighting for his life with an inexplicable, arthritis-like condition. From the pain and the fear over whether he would live or die came the realization that I could no longer rely just on my own strength. Chase's sudden, life-threatening illness forced me to rely on other men as never before—and on God like I'd never imagined.

That's where the spirit of God came in—where I first truly experienced a communion of fellowship, a body of believers who worshipped God in all aspects of their Christian lives. They say that spiritual lessons are repeated and intensified until they are learned. It felt like God kept upping the ante and allowed the pressure on me to increase until I recognized how much I needed Him—and how much I needed real connection and fellowship with other men.

My son's illness exposed a weakness in my own character that I had never paid attention to: my own tendency, rooted in my childhood, to close myself off to the help and friendship of my male peers. Even in the crucibles of manhood that war and pro football represent, I always kept my innermost self apart from my teammates and friends. I was trapped in the John Wayne myth our society embraces—that men must go it alone and that they cannot have deep friendships and meaningful bonds with other men. I never understood the importance of close male friendships, and how important they were to fulfilling my true potential as a man. I never understood what it meant to reach out to others and share with them at the deepest level my fears and my faith.

My son survived, but it has taken this continuing crisis to teach me that we all are created for relationships and that we're not meant to do life alone. Through all of these experiences, from the wrestling mat to the cockpit of an A-10, from the defensive line of the Cowboys to the emergency room of my son's hospital, I've learned that men need true friendship and accountability with other men, along with faith in God, if we are to be our best—or even if we just want to be happy. I want to share in this book the lessons I've learned as a fighter pilot, as a Cowboy, as a man of faith going through my son's illness, and in my involvement with at-risk kids and with amputees and sufferers of post-traumatic stress disorder (PTSD) returning from Iraq and Afghanistan.

The persistent go-it-alone myth in our society traps men from connecting in a meaningful way with other men. In all the roles I've been privileged to play in life, I've seen that men in our society are emotionally disconnected from each other and from God. But we *need* masculine relationships—friendships with other men, not just marriage and family. We need other men to hold us accountable in our actions and in our beliefs. The Bible calls David a "man after [God's] own heart" (1 Sam. 13:14 KJV). It makes sense that the man with the closest male friend in all of Scripture—Jonathan—is the man who pursues his relationship with God with his whole being. God uses our relationships with other men to reveal His character to us. These close friendships help us define who we're supposed to be: men. And not just men, but men after God's own heart.

It's never been so hard as in today's world to be a man because few of us have any idea about what a man's role is supposed to be. Touchy-feely? (Even beer ads mock men showing emotion.) Head of the household? Don't tell the feminists! Team player? (Not if getting ahead means beating the other guy, which so many people think is the ethos of the business world today.) In short, men are confused, and they're frustrated. We don't really know how we're supposed to function in the world today.

It's kind of ironic—we live in an age of tell-all daytime television shows, true confessions, and celebrities who are willing to admit to everything from mental illness to pornography addiction. But there's a difference between celebrities cashing in on their illnesses or weaknesses and true communication between real people. For the most part, real men—the people you see every day, at work, at church, at the gym—really have no one to talk to. Bruce Springsteen sang about having 57 channels on TV and nothing to watch. Today, we men possess the greatest communication devices in the history of mankind, from PDAs to the iPhone, but we're so stuck inside ourselves that we don't know how to communicate, or what, or to whom.

The importance of masculine relationships has diminished in modern society. We men have lost our masculine identities and we are playing roles in society today that are not in our character, not in our nature. I thought that manhood was an end in itself, that manhood was symbolized by success in wartime or in sports. But I now realize that manhood is the vehicle to the kind of life men are supposed to lead—where our most important missions are love of God, love of spouse, love of family, love of community, and love of country.

I've learned how to put down my armor and allow myself to reduce the angst and the stress I still deal with. I had to become more transparent, more open to others, more accountable, more willing to hold others accountable in their lives. I had to become more vulnerable and risk loss in order to heal the scars I had suffered as a boy. I no longer had to keep my personal armor up 24-7. Instead, I learned to put on the armor of God, because that is the source of my true strength.

It's about knowing God in my inner being, and this is only possible for me because I have come to know God deeply through the company of other men. For me, with my Christian walk, I always knew there was a God. But there's a difference between knowing it and KNOWING it. By deepening my relationships with other men, I have been able to deepen my relationship with God. Through trials, God pushed me to draw closer to Him, as my heavenly Father. He works through us and partners with us. But we need help, too, through our earthly friendships, to be good stewards, to stand up for truth and integrity. We are all a part of His body.

Men must be accountable to each other, because otherwise it's easy to let our own standards slip. We need affirmation from one another, because otherwise we may feel that our actions and hard work are simply disappearing in a void. We need acceptance from other men, sometimes to make up for the lack of acceptance we may have experienced from our fathers, and otherwise to satisfy the basic human craving for friendship and connection. I call Acceptance, Affirmation, and Accountability from other men the real AAA. It's the kind of roadside assistance no man should be without.

I want this book to make a difference, to tear down the walls that separate men from each other and from our true selves. I want to offer a plan for men that gives them an alternative to suffering in silence, feeling disconnected from their spouses and families, seeking to numb themselves through unhealthy coping mechanisms, whether it's alcohol, drugs, extramarital affairs, workaholism, addiction to pornography, prescription painkillers, or a combination thereof. A man's legacy must be more than killing time through work and killing pain through distraction. Men may be able to point with pride to their work, but what else in their lives do they have? If work is the only measure of a man's success, then the result is depression, disconnection, and at the extreme, even suicide.

I want men to find the joy and excitement in life that I have been privileged to experience in so many ways, public and private. This book is that plan. I have known the kind of friendships, mentoring relationships, and accountability rarely found in our society outside the arenas of war and sport. Again, it was never just about flying jets in combat or being a Super Bowl champion. As I said, I've always seen these experiences as preparation for something greater down the road. For me, that something is the ability to speak to men and inspire them to greatness, not just in their outer lives but in their hearts. Not just in their business dealings but in their marriages and in their relationships with their children. Not just in their workplaces but in their communities and in their country.

The plan I want to offer men comes in two parts. The first part, the first half of the book, will lay out the challenges men face on the inside, in their own hearts. The true measure of manhood is not accomplishment but character and meaning. In this half of the book, I want to share with men what I have learned about what we need on the inside, in order to solidify our own identities and discover who we are really meant to be. It's about crafting character and casting a vision, healing the troubled past, developing a work ethic, committing to a balance of self, finding fulfillment, and living your spirituality. You may recognize these as the chapter titles of the first part of this book. That's because each of these lessons can stand alone as one part of your mission to living a meaningful life.

I think of the first half of the book as basic training. I know a little bit about basic training after having gone through intense training for the Air Force and training camp with the Dallas Cowboys—where I would typically lose fourteen pounds every single day and have to gain it back. Add up all the days I was in training camp for the Cowboys and that comes out to over a year of my life. So I do know about what it takes to train with the best—to be the best.

Part II of the book is Active Duty—how we conduct ourselves when we're on the battlefield, whether the field is our home, our workplace, our community, our country, or our relationship with God. This is where we will talk about moving past the cultural facade that we men erect for ourselves. I want to share what I have learned about making a strategic plan for one's life, about serving the family, about developing true friendships with other men, about the real role of work and money in men's lives, about the importance of community service, and, ultimately, about redefining male success in today's world.

I guess you could say that the first half of this book discusses the core competencies that a man needs in order to succeed today, and the second half shows how to put those core competencies into action.

In the Air Force, I often heard it said that the rules of engagement—the guidelines for combat and engaging the enemy—were "written in blood." That's because someone lost his life learning a lesson that the rest of us now have a rule to go by. One such rule preached to us from day one was this: take care of your wingman, the plane flying adjacent to yours as you go into combat. If you don't take care of your wingman, your chances of getting shot down go way up and your chances of completing your mission go way down.

We weren't meant to go it alone, but most men labor under the misapprehension that it is unmanly to ask for help. My years in the Air Force cemented in my mind that, on the contrary, nothing is more important than the relationship between a flight lead and his wingman. During the first Gulf War, I once knew a pilot who had to eject from his fighter jet in close proximity to the enemy. His wingman stayed in the vicinity to keep the bad guys away until the helicopters could come and rescue him. The lesson I took from this event was that when we find ourselves in enemy territory where we are tempted to do something not in keeping with our values or vows, sometimes we do stumble and sometimes we do fall. As Galatians 6:1 reminds us, it's the job of our wingman to restore us to God's purpose for our lives. Women don't know this side of men—because we don't talk about it. Maybe because we *can't* talk about it—we know that something's wrong but we just can't find the words to describe what it is.

As a three-time NFL world champion, I can assure you that individuals don't win football games, let alone Super Bowls. Teams do. And yet, despite all evidence that teamwork, togetherness, and trust are the foundation of true success, in today's world, men remain isolated, stuck, unable even to tell each other the truth about how they feel about marriage, work, money, religion, or practically any subject of importance.

Someone might read these words and say, "How unmanly!" I would argue that there is nothing more manly than connecting in a deep, meaningful way with one's fellow man, in the world of sports, in business, in the community, in church, and in our families.

So who are we men on the inside? Are we John Wayne? John Bradshaw? John Gray (author of *Men Are from Mars, Women Are from Venus*)? Are we some combination thereof? Or, are we something else altogether?

And what are the rules of engagement by which we are meant to live?

As the pilot of an A-10 in wartime, we would never go into combat without a clear plan so that we knew our objective, the terrain, the threats, and the climate. And since the key to airpower is flexibility, we also had to know how to make appropriate changes literally on the fly as new situations developed. You could call this book a flight plan or a game plan for life—whatever the metaphor, it's what men lack, and it's what men need. These are the Rules of Engagement, the plan for a new kind of manhood. And it's what I believe I have been called to share with men.

PART I

Basic Training: Your Foundation

CHAPTER ONE

Crafting Character and Casting a Vision

My friend Michael Irvin, who has been through his share of trials and tribulations and who today is a powerful man of faith, tells the story that when he was playing, everybody shouted at him, "You da Man!" And he thought to himself, "If I'm 'da Man,' what is 'da Man' supposed to do?"

Well, the answer is obvious—if everybody's expecting you to play a certain role, then go play it! And being "da Man" meant lots of women, lots of flair, lots of drugs, and ultimately, lots of trouble.

And then, Michael says, he had a conversion experience and he suddenly realized that he wasn't "da Man"—instead, he was a man. Now he was confronted with a new question: what does it mean to be a man? And suddenly a whole new range of answers came into view for him. A man is supposed to be honest. A man is supposed to be faithful. A man is supposed to be fair. A man is supposed to set a good example. A man is supposed to think of others and not just himself.

Everybody remembers the headlines about Michael Irvin from a few years back, but he is a changed man. Why? Because he went from being "da Man" to being "a man."

Character is the foundation for a successful life. We have to know who we are, what we are, and what we stand for before we can go out into the world and accomplish anything of importance, from marriage and family to success in the workplace or the sports arena. Character means recognizing both our strengths and our shortcomings, acknowledging our failures, and developing humility to make better decisions. As Colin Wilson, author of *Religion and the Rebel*, says, "a visionary disciplines himself always to see the world as if for the first time." We men must play the role of visionaries in our own lives, taking a moment to stop and see who we are, what we are, and what we can become. We have all too often compromised our character not out of weakness or poor judgment but because we didn't see the value in living according to the way we know we should.

As I was putting this book together, I found myself confronting the theme of character over and over. In fact it's one of the central messages of this book. A man's character is paramount to who he is—especially who he is as a man of God. Because I am convinced that a man's character is at the core of the Rules of Engagement by which we're meant to live, we're going to discuss it in depth.

Defining Character

Character is your core integrity. It's made up of your core values and beliefs. Character doesn't necessarily revolve around doctrinal belief. It's not about what denomination you belong to, what the belief system of that denomination is, or how you go about defining yourself in religious terms. As a Christian, all things are irrelevant if you do not have a personal relationship with Jesus Christ. Now, what does that mean? It means that Christ, if you believe what it says in the Bible, was sent by God, who recognized that man could not live up to the law of the Old Testament. Jesus recognized that God was trying to reveal Himself to us in the law, and that if we followed His Commandments, we would be all right.

But it's not that simple. Even to the best of our ability as human beings, we're never going to be able to live up to that expectation. We can't. Only God can because only God is great—He's perfect, in that He can do no sin. That's why God sent Christ as His sacrifice for us. Christ shed His blood on the cross for us as believers, and that's the whole aspect of grace. Everything starts and ends with belief.

In today's world, the concept of grace is so foreign to us that we have trouble opening up to receive it. Ultimately, though, it's just a matter of accepting what God wants us to have. We think we have to do X, Y, and Z, or that we have to do penance, but that's already been paid for. The price has already been paid, and as a result, we have true freedom. That's the cornerstone of faith.

So a man's relationship to himself begins with the relationship to his God. It's not a matter of following certain rules or going to a certain church or "making yourself good," because you can never be good in an absolute sense. No matter how hard you try, no matter how much discipline you have in your life, you'll never measure up. No man has ever measured up to God. That's when we come to the realization that it's not about us. It's about how we fit into the grand scheme of this thing called life. The vision of how we fit in is an extension of our character.

When I was at the Air Force Academy, a Medal of Honor winner from the Vietnam era came and spoke to us. One of the most profound things that I heard him discuss was how his experience of Vietnam translated from the battlefield into the rest of his life. Today he is a real estate developer. He said that he learned in battle that if you couldn't trust your peers in battle, you couldn't accomplish your mission. All I have is my word. All I have is my character. If I compromise that, I'll never gain it back. It's gone forever. It's as true in business as it is in war that you have to be able to trust, and if you're going to trust, you have to be trustworthy as well.

Character is not a thing you can turn on and off. It's not a light switch. It's more than just a choice—it's a way of life. Character is formulated in you beginning from the day you were born. It defines who you are as an individual. It's about making choices. It's not something you just read about in a textbook, or even in a book like this. It's something you pave with your thoughts, your words, and your actions. It's pragmatic. It's how you lead your life.

> Character is not a thing you can turn on and off. It's not a light switch. It's more than just a choice—it's a way of life.

What does it mean if I believe that a man has strong character? Well, he's showing me a number of things. He's showing me that I can trust him, that his word is good enough for me. It means that his outlook on life isn't just about material gain or about making a dollar. Instead, it's about "How can I help you?"—because that man knows that the hand most often to give is most open to receive.

Character is about the giving of self, service before self, which is one of the models of all our service academies. Service above self means the ability to put yourself in harm's way or give of yourself where it may cost you something, but you do it anyway, because it's the right thing. If I'm evaluating an individual, whether I'm going into business, battle, or athletic competition with that person, I want to know what his primary focus in life is. Is he all about himself, or is he about service? Would I trust him in a foxhole? Would I trust him looking after my back? Would I trust him looking after my family if something happened to me? Can I implicitly trust that individual, or do I need a tight contract, with nondisclosure and noncircumvent clauses before I would ever do any business with that individual? Bottom line: can I take that man's word as his bond? Those are the things that define character for me. From that flows out all the ancillary things about trustworthiness, about ethics, about all the other things associated with living a life of character.

It may be all but impossible to create character under fire. Ideally, we take time to consider and create our character before the battle begins, and then conflict becomes a test of our character, a proven ground for it, instead of a place to develop it. In other words, when you enter the arena, whether we're talking about sports, war, business, or your private life, you better come to the situation armed with the kind of character that will get you through it.

In the military, you train to go to war. In any sport, you practice long before the first game. You train to play in that game, but you never really know you've got what it takes, or how you'll measure up, until you get that first hit in a football game, or you face live pitching in a baseball game, or face live fire in a combat mission. Everything up until that point has just been practice. It's just been theory. Pragmatic application is where the rubber meets the road. You can read as many books as you want on character and you can read as many things as you want about the great men and women who have served our country. But they never knew what they had until they were tested under fire. At some point, we are all going to be tested. Whether you're facing combat, bankruptcy, or foreclosure, or you're in a relationship and you have a temptation to cheat on your wife or look at pornography, the one thing I can guarantee you about life is that you will be tested.

There's an example from my own life of a time I was tested under fire. After I'd been playing professional football for a few years, my wife and I decided to build a home in Colorado. We were halfway through the construction process when our son's illness took a turn for the worse and we would not be able to move to Colorado. Suddenly, I was sinking all this money into a house that there was no way we could move into. We knew we had to sell the property, but nobody was buying. In fact we still have the house today—we've been searching for a buyer for four years. As you might imagine, I've sunk a ton of money into that house.

In the midst of all of this, we were trying to seek financing to take some of the strain off. At one point, the mortgage officer said to me, "Look, just say it's your primary residence. Don't worry about it." And I said to him, "No, I can't do that. It's not right." In the meantime, I was getting killed on the insurance. If I'd lied and said it was a primary residence instead of a rental property, things would have been a lot easier. But I couldn't do it. So to all the people who were wheeling and dealing to try and save me money, I told them I'd rather take the hit.

We've had that house for a while now and it's cost me a lot of money. Some people have even said to me, "Just give it back to the bank, Chad, and stop worrying about it." But that just wouldn't be right. I made a commitment to do everything within my means, and I'll keep trying to sell the house until it sells or I run out of money.

Am I losing money? You bet I am. But did I make the right choice? There's not a doubt in my mind that I did. Not only did I keep my spiritual slate clean, but I made a decision that was pragmatic, too. I could have gotten in a whole lot of trouble for claiming that house as my primary residence when it wasn't. Instead, I stayed true to my character. And now I'm not sitting here wondering how I'll look in stripes.

So the essence of character is this: What do you do when the lights are out? What do you do when nobody's looking at you? Are you going to be the same person? Are you going to follow through and do what's right? What's right is universal truth, it isn't situational. We live in an era when people believe that there are no such things as right and wrong. I completely disagree. There are no gray areas when it comes to truth.

The beginning of wisdom is recognizing that truth exists,

and molding ourselves to fit the truth, instead of molding reality to fit our transient desires.

The need to develop character starts young. It's not just when you turn eighteen and you go to college or enter a military academy or go into the service or get a job. It goes all the way back to your first party in high school. How are you going to react to a compromising situation if you haven't thought things through beforehand? Because one thing is certain: you *will* go through the crucible. This means you have to be ready to go through it the right way.

Pitching Out of the Fight

We live in an era when we're totally inundated from the media about how to think and act. You can get instantaneous access to anything on the Internet, and that includes access to belief systems, different perspectives, different spins on things. That means people can get their outlook on life from any source other than those that matter the most—the Bible, the church, and especially, the family.

We live in an era with a lack of role modeling by our fathers. In our society, there is a 50-plus percent divorce rate. In the African-American community, 70 percent of children are raised by their mothers in a single-parent setting. In too many families today, there is no role modeling whatsoever on the part of fathers. There's no balance, because it takes a mother and a father to raise a family. You need the father's masculine side to offset the mother's nurturing side. God is both masculine and feminine.

He created the marriage unit to be both of those things, to have both the masculine and the feminine. One-half to two-thirds of society, or more, is raising their children without that sense of balance, and we see the disastrous results every day.

Fathers have abdicated their responsibilities to their sons in all too many cases. Fathers have checked out, quite frankly. They haven't shown their kids the right way. We may tell our kids, "Don't drink alcohol, don't drink beer, don't drink and drive." But when they see Dad coming home from work, he's got a beer in his hand, and then he jumps behind the wheel. I call that checking out.

We fathers are not taking the God-given role that God gave us, to be the heads and leaders of our families. That doesn't mean that we're supposed to be dominant over our wives. Couples have to make decisions on a mutual basis. So what is the father's role? To cast the vision for his family. You as a father have to define for yourself who you are and what you believe before you can give your family a clear direction. That's why knowing yourself, and knowing your relationship with Jesus Christ, is the starting point. Because otherwise, if you don't have guidelines or rules of engagement for yourself, how can you possibly play a leadership role in your own home?

At some point in our culture, the father's role changed from being the mentor, being the rock, the foundation of the family, casting the vision, and "naming" his kids. Today, however, the attitude is, "I just need to provide material things for my family. My kids have all the blessings of life. They live in a good house. That's my job. I'm done."

We fathers haven't followed up on the most important thing, which is mentoring our children and helping them define who they are as Christians. We need them to know not only who they are, but who they are and who they need to be in Christ. And that can happen only if we know who we are and who we need to be.

Why have fathers checked out?

Back in the day, prior to the Industrial Revolution, a father and his sons would be together all day. The kids would go out into the field with the dad and they would work. Or a son would be an apprentice for his father, whether his father was a butcher or a shoemaker or a miller. So the father would spend all day with his sons. They would talk about things, and he would be hands-on, showing his sons how to work. This is how this is done. This is why we do this. They would have conversations.

A great example of this is my father and his father. My dad spent some fifty-odd years working on our family farm with my grandfather. Every day, they were talking, sharing, and learning together. Their relationship was so close. I'm envious of that. My brother has carried on that tradition. He works on the farm with my dad, and they spend every day together talking about all kinds of things.

Now, with the advent of technology, families don't live in that manner. Families are spread out. Fathers don't necessarily work on their farm, or in their home. They work in the city. They commute, or they travel, and they're able to provide a very good means for their family, but they can't, don't, or won't spend adequate time with their kids.

My father taught my brother and all of us, up until the point that I moved away, what it means to be a farmer, and to learn and to grow. Farmers don't just grow crops—we grow ourselves. My father showed his weaknesses and his strengths and how to overcome adversity. What it all came down to was time—quality and quantity time, and that's what he gave all of us. I took a different path in my life, going first into the military and then into pro football. So I did not have some of the formative experiences with my father that my brother enjoyed. But I developed enough of a foundation from my father to understand who I am—who I am in the world, and who I am in Christ. Many sons don't have that opportunity, because their fathers have simply checked out.

Today, the focus has changed in our society for men. We are no longer expected to provide a *life* for the members of our family—a financial living, a material living, certainly, but never an inner life or a spiritual life. Men today are expected to provide a living, but not a life. When a man makes a living, he makes available to his family food, shelter, and clothing. But when he offers his family a life, he provides not just for his material things. He also provides a spiritual foundation and a sense of balance.

We men are caught today in a dilemma. On the one hand, society tells us to seek immediate gratification in whatever form that may take, at whatever cost we and others we love might pay. If marriage is disposable, and if I have only one life to live, then why can't I do what I want with whom I want whenever I want? The other side of the coin for men is deferred joy—the statement that always begins, "I'll be happy when." As in, I'll be happy when the kids graduate, when I get that promotion, when I get that raise, when I retire."

> When we develop and define our character, it will make it more difficult for us to take the easy road out and "check out" of the calling God has for each of us.

We men lull ourselves to sleep with the false promise of "I'll be happy when"—and then we wake up decades later with nothing to show for our lives but a 401(k) if we're lucky. Somewhere between the constraints, and I truly see them as constraints, of immediate gratification and deferred joy is a life of true meaning, service, commitment, growth, and accomplishment. And the foundation stone of all these things is character. When we develop and define our character, it will make it more difficult for us to take the easy road out and "check out" of the calling God has for each of us.

Casting Your Vision

During my time in the NFL, I was certainly tempted by the promise of free agency and the income boost it would bring. But I felt a commitment to the Dallas Cowboys, who had taken a chance on me, and I also felt a commitment to my wife and children, not to tear them away from the roots that they had established in their own lives. I like what the golfer Chi Chi Rodriguez says— "What you take with you is what you leave behind." Otherwise, if all we have to show after a lifetime is a positive balance sheet, what were we? There'll be a tombstone in the cemetery—"Here lies John Doe. Here lies John—and here lies his dough."

People say to me all the time, "Chad, what do you know

about the struggles that men face? You have succeeded at everything you've done!" My response is that I've been very fortunate in terms of the results I have achieved, but we all face the same battles, whether it's the impetus to cheat on our wives or cheat on our taxes. Character in my mind is defined as what you do when no one else is looking. Don't you think men in the military and members of even the best organizations in the NFL are exposed to temptation every day? You better believe it! And I was not perfect. I was always true to my marriage vows, but like all fighter pilots, I tried to live up to the expectation of work hard—and party even harder! What I've learned is that we're not called upon to be perfect. Instead, we're called upon to believe and trust in the Perfect One.

Every man comes to a point in his life where he asks, "What is this all about? Who am I? Where am I going?" That moment came for me when I'd been playing in the NFL for nine years. I was only thirty-six years old, and suddenly I was looking at my life and wrestling with the big questions of who I was. "*Now* what were my next steps? Where did I fit? What would define me now?" All of these questions were whirling around in my head at the speed of light. And in the midst of it all, I cried out, "God, who am I supposed to be? Who did you *create* me to be?"

That's the moment I realized that all my accomplishments, all my various past titles, were only things I had done. They didn't define me as an individual. Up to that point, they had been my defining experiences. But in reality they were only steps on the way to defining my purpose. Today, I feel I know what that purpose is, the real reason God put me on this Earth—to relate to other people, and to be able to speak and motivate and lead others. It's not about the things we do in this world. It's about our attitude toward God and how we can serve Him.

Sure, we all have to make practical decisions in our lives, and there are certain accomplishments we all strive for—things we know we're supposed to do, like finishing high school or getting a job. But in addition to those basic life decisions, you have to find who you are as an individual. Otherwise, you'll be lost. You've got to lay that foundation of character first. That's what I call casting your vision. This vision is also where God's will for your life comes into play. And as the book of Proverbs tells us, "Where there is no vision, the people perish" (Prov. 29:18 KJV).

———·———

Character and vision go hand in hand, because a man's vision comes directly from his character. And casting your personal vision is essential. Your vision is your compass—it will keep you headed in the right direction when the temptations of the world try to push you off course.

A vision for one's life isn't just a goal or a milestone as in "I want to go to college" or "I want to be on the team" or "I want to get the promotion." It's about setting in concrete who we are. A solid foundation for a man might include these statements: I believe in God. I believe there's a difference between right and wrong. I believe that there is a universal truth. I believe that I'm created in God's image. These are the core values by which a man needs to live.

A strong physical core is the foundation of physical fitness. You're only as strong as your core—the muscle group around your abdomen that is the first to fire when you are doing any movement, lifting weights, running, or doing anything at all. Strong core, strong body. Weak core, weak body. A weak core often leads to injury. The same thing is true with a strong core vision. This is what defines who you are as an individual—and it's all about what you believe. Life will be that much easier for you when you have clear core values, solid core strength. It creates strong guidelines: If something does not mesh with your core vision of yourself, your basic values as to who you are, don't do it. Just don't do it.

Unfortunately, this philosophy doesn't fit into today's postmodern thought process. Today, men define themselves based on a whim or an emotion, and they redefine that vision depending on the situation. Every time we redefine the truth about ourselves, we chip away at the truth until there's no core left. And as the expression goes, if you don't stand for something, you'll fall for anything.

In any negotiation, from a business deal to diplomacy, if you don't have a common ground on which to negotiate, you're lost. You can't get anywhere because you don't have a common vision or a common core. I believe that truth is truth, and that there is universal truth, which are the truths by which we men are meant to live our lives. The term I use for those universal truths is "rules of engagement." Sound familiar?

From a military perspective, when you break one of the rules of engagement, it's going to cost you something important. It can cost you your life, your relationships, or your integrity. It can cost you your position in culture and society, the way people view you. When you bust it, there's a cost. We've all seen leading members of society brought down in a heartbeat from their important positions because they lack that sense of core integrity. We see it in the headlines, and we also see it in our communities—men who apply "situational ethics," whatever that means, instead of universal truths. They cheat on their taxes, their business partners, and their wives. And they end up paying a terrible price. All because they hadn't taken the time to define their core values and commit to live by them. Before you can pass on anything to your children, your peers, or society, you must know who you are and you must know what you hold to be truth. That comes first, before you can do anything else.

It's all about taking care of self. Who are you as an individual? What are you? Life isn't easy. You will inevitably find yourself confronted by a serious challenge—a health issue, the health of a child, a relationship problem, or a job issue where you're facing financial turmoil, or some other aspect of pain or strife in your life. These situations can trigger a crisis of belief. From a faith-based perspective, it's a gut-check moment. It's when you ask yourself, "Do I believe what God says to be true? Do I believe what He says about me? Do I believe the foundational truths set down from day one, since the creation of the world? Do I believe what the Bible says about our relationship as Christians with Jesus Christ? Do I believe all that to be true?"

It's through the pain process that we do the soul-searching necessary to look at our own lives and continue to define and

18

refine who we are. Those kinds of personal crises I mentioned a moment ago are typically the catalyst for a crisis of belief. The good news is that you don't have to go through that crisis of faith. When you go through personal pain, it refines your faith just as metal is refined when it passes through a hot flame. If you stop before the crisis inevitably occurs and take time to define your core values, they will be in place, clearly delineated and ready to operate when challenges arrive.

Without a doubt, the biggest crisis I've faced was my son's illness. Up to that point in my life, I'd never really been challenged in my beliefs. But as my wife, Tammy, and I struggled through the health of our child, we were wading through all sorts of conflicting theologies. People told us to pray. To fast. To anoint Chase with oil. Like any parents would, we tried everything. But Chase continued to get worse.

The questions I kept asking were: God, I know You're real—but why? Why are we going through this? What does it mean? This little boy didn't do anything. There were times my wife and I literally cried out, "Please, God, punish us!" We figured if anything, we were the sinners. Our two-year-old was innocent. Why did God allow this to happen to him? Every day the overwhelming pain made it a huge challenge for us to really search the scriptures, to pray, and to seek who God is yesterday, today, and tomorrow.

Scripture says His ways are not our ways, nor His thoughts our thoughts (see Isa. 55:8). The way we want our life to be is not necessarily what God has in store for us. I firmly believe that all things work for the good of those who love God and are called according to His purpose. Of course when you're faced with the potential death of your child, it's a little harder to understand that. That period in our lives was truly a crisis of belief for my wife and me. It forced us to ask ourselves: Do we really believe that God is sovereign? That He is in control and all around us when we feel so helpless, so hopeless? When we can't find any medical answers to help our son?

God gives grace, but it takes our faith to be able to put it into practice. For those who lack a clearly defined vision, who don't have that clearly defined set of core values about who they are as individuals, they can be like a rudderless ship at sea, just tossed about. Because of our foundation of faith, my wife and I made it through that crisis, our belief in God even stronger than before. And He blessed us by taking Chase in His arms and holding him close. God saved my son when he was at his worst.

Building Your Foundation

In the New Testament, Jesus talks about building your house upon the rock or upon the sand. He who builds his house upon the rock, upon the truth, doesn't have to worry about what storm or tempest will come through. He knows he'll get beat upon, but he also knows he's strong and stable. All will be well. For those who build their home upon the sand, the foundation will not hold because there is no foundation.

When is it best to take time out from your daily activities to build this foundation? To define your core values and cast your vision? There's that line about when it's time to open your parachute when you're skydiving—when the people look like ants, it's too soon, and when the ants look like people, it's too late. Maybe a better comparison is the question of when to take out insurance. They say it's better to take it out a year too soon than a moment too late. And that's how it is with taking time to define our core values. The best time to do it is *right now*. It doesn't matter if you're young or if you're later in life. It's only too late when you're dead.

In his play *Broadway Bound*, the playwright Neil Simon depicts a father who realizes the high cost he has paid for failing to define his own core values. The father tells his son, "I thought wisdom comes with age. It doesn't. Wisdom comes with wisdom." In other words, defining one's values isn't something that happens by itself. Instead, it's a process to which we must devote ourselves, or it will never happen.

Fortunately, the process is simpler than one might imagine. It's really just about asking yourself a series of simple questions:

- Imagine looking back from your deathbed upon your life; are you satisfied with what you see?
- Why do you make your living as you do? Are you doing what you do for money, for fame, for status, for your family?
- Where do you see yourself down the road?
- Where do you want to be?
- How do you see yourself currently? What are your strengths?
- What are your weaknesses?
- Who do you want to be?

For me it has always been all about training. This is just as true in one's private life and one's professional career as it is in the Air Force or on the football field. The good news is that you don't have to come up with all the training lessons yourself. Learn from others and then come up with your own strategic plan.

Sometimes you hear people say that you need to make God a priority in your life. Well, if you think that way, God will be just a portion of your day. He'll be perhaps thirty minutes out of your morning, when you are in prayer or quiet time, and the rest of the time is with your family, with your work, with your extracurricular activities, your recreation, or whatever else you like to do. And God will be apart from all that. But, in fact, God needs to be a part of everything. He's in you. He's a part of all those things. Saint Paul said when you pray, pray continuously (see 1 Thess. 5:17). It doesn't mean saying, "Okay, I'm going to do fifteen minutes of quiet time right now and then I'll forget about God the rest of the day."

Your relationship with God is continuous. It's about balance. It's about balance between the four areas of life—the physical, the mental, the commitment to family, and the commitment to community. Jesus Christ is at the center of that. I use the analogy of the cross because in the Christian faith, Christ is right in the middle of all that. That's how you determine your balance. That's what determines your vision and your value system, your core. Everything revolves around that. That's where you

> Your relationship with God is continuous.

start, recognizing that your relationship with self begins with your relationship with Christ. Before you can have any relationships with anybody else, you have to first have that relationship with Christ. You have to define who you are as an individual based on that. You're not meant to John Wayne it. No one can survive on his own for long. You may be successful for a period of time, but, ultimately, the things of this world are going to weigh you down and eventually take you out. You'll burn out. That's the price we pay for ignoring the Rules of Engagement.

The Importance of Role-Playing

I'm a big believer in role-playing. What happens if you're a teenager, or even if you're in your twenties or thirties, and you're at a party, and someone hands you something you don't recognize and says, "Here, try this. It will be good"? Unless you've actually role-played and walked through that, you're going to be shooting from the hip. That may be a fifty-fifty proposition—how you react under peer pressure. But if you've already thought through that process, you know how you're going to react. That's your battle plan. That's your game plan. Those are your rules of engagement.

The same thing is true if you're going for your appointment with your tax attorney or your CPA. He might say, "If we take this little deduction here, it's borderline, but I think I can defend you on that." What do you do? Do you take the attitude of "I'll let the IRS come after me"? Or do you do the right thing from the start?

If you open up an e-mail from a friend and he's sent you a

link to an Internet porn site, what do you do? Do you delete it right away? Or do you follow the link?

Unless you role-play, you put yourself in harm's way. That's where you have to make those decisions beforehand, before you get to the game, the battle, the Web site, the party, or the appointment with your accountant. That's where your rules of engagement come in. You role-play. You think things through. Then, when you get in the first game, even before you take your first hit, you know exactly how you're going to react.

Building a Legacy

What's true wealth? Your vision. What determines your legacy? Again, it's your vision. Your legacy is not simply about riches and material things. Those things can be gone tomorrow, as a lot of people are experiencing during this economic crisis. Your wealth can be gone tomorrow, but the things that last throughout the generations are your vision and your character. That's true wealth. Character is forged from your decisions, and it's the true wealth that you pass on to your children. That's what transcends generations. As it says in Proverbs, a good name is better than silver or gold (see Prov. 22:1).

And yet, we live in a time when people are not interested in crafting a vision for their lives. Instead, as I said earlier, everything is situational. Men think they can be ready for Mrs. Right when they're spending the night with Ms. Right Now. But there's an old adage that a football coach once told me: it only catches up to you when it catches up to you, and it always catches up to you.

Every weekend, or even multiple times throughout the week when I was at the Air Force Academy, I'd be getting drunk with the boys, pounding the beers, chasing women, the whole thing. Back then, I felt I needed to create that immediate gratification. That's the whole thing—we men want that bandage. We want that placebo. We think that's what we need, but the next day we wake up and we realize—and I speak from experience—that there is shame. There is guilt. There is a huge vacuum inside us that we fail to fill with hedonistic activities.

Blaise Pascal, the French mathematician and philosopher, wrote that inside of every man is a God-sized vacuum that only God can fill. That's why we have to ask ourselves: What is our purpose in life? Why are we doing what we're doing? Everybody wants great relationships. We all want to be loved, and every man wants to live a life of significance. We want to have a purpose, a passion, the ability to go out and conquer, to subdue.

We cannot do it on our own—it has to be all about God. That's where character comes in—it's the realization that (a) it's not about you, (b) it's making good decisions, and (c) you can't do it on your own. You need God in your life. You need others to support you, and it's a lifelong process.

It's not about being perfect, because there's only One who is perfect. But unless we have character and make the right decisions, we'll be extremely susceptible to whatever comes along. If you cannot consistently make good decisions, either in your personal life or in your workplace, and unless you've got God at the center of your life, you'll be susceptible to following that same slippery slope of addiction and bad choices. You'll be able to rationalize anything, and one day you'll wake up and say, "God, how did I ever get where I am right now?"

If you're at that point right now, rest assured: it's never too late. God's still waiting for you, and He loves you as much as He always did. As the expression goes, if you feel distance from God, who moved?

When you develop your character, the upside is that you're playing on the right team. You've got better teammates. You feel connected. You're making better choices. It gets easier. Here's the kicker: one bad decision can possibly throw you back down, but through forgiving yourself, getting on your knees, and asking God to help you again, you can go right back to where you were before. God always forgives, no matter what you do, but you do have to ask Him to help you find victory.

When you play football, your team can be down, but if you and your teammates are of the never-give-up variety, you'll say, "Hey, we just need to put two or three wins together." That's how the 2007 Giants were. They lost their first couple of games, and then they went on an incredible roll, because they believed in themselves. They were not the most talented team on paper, but they beat three truly outstanding teams—my own Dallas Cowboys, the Green Bay Packers with Brett Favre, and then the undefeated New England Patriots—to become the Super Bowl champions. Games aren't won on paper any more than wars are. Life doesn't happen on paper. It happens when we're in the arena, being tested, and making sure that we don't give in and we don't give up.

Before we can be of any use to anyone else, we have to make

ourselves useful to God. The way we do that is that we accept Him into our lives, let Him know that we are willing to go to any lengths for victory, whether it's in the battlefield, on the football field, the workplace, or our homes. Again, I'm talking about winning ethically, because winning by any other means is just another form of defeat. It catches up to you when it catches up to you, and it will always catch up to you. Conversely, when you make strong character the definition of who you are as a person, and when you commit yourself to yourself and to God, anything good can happen. And it surely will.

CHAPTER TWO

Healing the Troubled Past

Everybody has a story. I don't care who you are. Everybody has some issue in their life that they're dealing with, and there's a story that goes along with that. Stories can be small or great, long lasting or recent, physical or spiritual. We all have something in our past that we're not proud of—a past indiscretion, sin, or weakness. The shameful event might be something as small as having stolen bubble gum from the corner store when you were a kid, or as large as having committed a heinous crime. Sometimes our troubled past is a result of the actions of others, such as through child abuse. But no matter what size or form it takes, we all have a story, and before we can move on and write the next successful chapter in our lives, we have to come to terms with our past.

So often, we men feel such shame over earlier actions that we remain trapped in the past, unable to confront the present or envision a more meaningful future. I hear of this corrosive, all-powerful shame from soldiers returning from Iraq, where they had to shoot at women or children strapped with bombs in order to protect themselves and their fellow soldiers. But I also hear of this shame from men here at home. It's the shame of a husband who has been unfaithful in his marriage vows and doesn't feel worthy of a second chance. It's the same shame that keeps a drug addict mired in the haze of the most recent high, or the sex addict focused on Internet pornography and prostitutes.

———·———

We men have forgotten who we are.

Post-traumatic stress disorder (PTSD), which afflicts an increasing number of veterans returning from combat in Iraq, has been the inability to process through, and to come to terms with, the experiences to ourselves or those close to us. A part of this can be a loss of identity. Why do the toughest of the tough— Marine Recons, Navy Seals, Green Beret paratroopers, Army Rangers, i.e., the ultimate masculine men—continue to re-enlist time and again, putting their lives on the line even after they've fulfilled their commitment to their country?

One reason might be that ingrained in the heart of every man is the commandment, thou shalt not murder. And by having killed, these men feel they have lost a sense of innocence that they hope to retrieve by returning to the battlefield, as if lost innocence were something that could be reclaimed as easily as a lost wallet. Only in battle, they believe, can they find their lost innocence and release the pictures that they see in their heads.

For many men, returning to a sin—going back to the bottle, continuing an extramarital affair, revisiting a pornographic Web site—is a way to find a lost identity. The last time they visited each of these places, they lost something of themselves, and they return in an attempt to find fulfillment in reclaiming what was lost. The behavior soon becomes a crutch, and eventually a poison that destroys the soul.

Each of us is imperfect, and we cannot overcome this world through our actions or disciplines alone. Instead, we must rely upon a higher power to survive. No one has ever overcome a true addiction through his own discipline, so we must turn to Christ to aid us in this endeavor. Then we must turn to the body of Christ: our fellowship of male believers.

In the previous chapter, we talked about casting your vision as a man of God. But many men are so bogged down by the shame, guilt, and heavy issues of their pasts that they are unable to project into the future and envision a great life for themselves. In this chapter, I want to explore how to move past the shame, how to rediscover the worthiness that resides in the hearts of men, so that you can reconnect with the Godly spark within and the vision of who you were always meant to be.

Exposing It to the Light

If you want to get free and heal your troubled past, the true freedom comes with what we have in Christ. We must first allow ourselves to be vulnerable and admit our mistakes. I call this process "exposing it to the light." When you keep secrets locked deep within, they only

> When you keep secrets locked deep within, they only increase the darkness in your heart.

increase the darkness in your heart. By exposing them to the light—first confessing them to God and then by sharing your sins with those close to you—you begin the process of freeing that shame and guilt, which is the first step on the road to recovery. "Therefore submit to God. Resist the devil and he will flee from you" (James 4:7 NKJV).

Unfortunately, most men feel the need to prove their machismo, even to themselves. They tell themselves they're disciplined enough to handle a "little" temptation. But it takes a far stronger man to admit his weakness than it does to yield to a vice. Strength is derived from limiting our weaknesses, which means we must strive for victory over our past troubles. Most men believe that a facade of strength is adequate replacement for real strength, and that appearing powerful to others is equivalent to possessing that actual power.

This inability to admit weakness results in superficial, and often dishonest, relationships between men. If you can't admit your weaknesses to your friends, not only can they not help in providing their outside strength, but you're actually eroding the potential of that strength by building a false foundation.

Exposing to the light doesn't bring about immediate healing. It's but the first step on a road as long as your troubles are great. Sometimes Christians do their faith a disservice by painting a rosy picture about Christianity being the end to all problems—that accepting the Lord guarantees health, happiness, and prosperity. But that's as far from the truth as you can get.

We have to remember the various stories in the Bible where men of faith found comfort in suffering. During the many years

David was hunted by Saul, God was always with David. Joseph spent years as a slave and then imprisoned by the Egyptians, throughout which time the Lord continually remained with Joseph—who went on to govern Egypt for Pharaoh.

A pastor friend of mine made an analogy of the baggage we as Christians carry. Imagine two TSA lines at the airport, one for those who have accepted Christ and the other for those who have rejected Him. Those in the rejection line are laden with an assortment of baggage, from small attaché cases to giant steamer trunks. The baggage represents traumas that a troubled past still causes in their lives.

Now let's say that one of the individuals in the rejection line makes a profession of faith in Christ and moves to the other line. Does he leave his baggage there? No. He brings his entire luggage collection with him. He joins the others in this line of salvation who also have luggage from past and current sins and indiscretions. His eternal life is now secure, but he's still accountable for his past thoughts and deeds, whether great or minor.

The Loss of Identity

Throughout our lives, we learn and heed the commandment "Thou shalt not murder." When men go into combat, they're faced with the contrary notions of obeying this commandment and following their commander's orders. Research has shown that prior to World War II, only 18–20 percent of troops expended ordnance with intent to kill. That means that at least 80 percent either fired over the heads of the enemy or didn't engage at all. Though they were on the front line directly in harm's way, they couldn't pull the trigger, even to protect their own skin.

Soon thereafter, military training evolved to become more realistic, with soldiers shooting at human silhouettes rather than bull's-eyes. Repetitive exposure to shooting at lifelike forms as well as other types of training led to soldiers becoming desensitized once they reached the battlefield. By the time of the Vietnam War, the percentage of soldiers who aimed with intent to kill rose into the high-90-percent area.

We each have our own perceptions of ourselves. But how do others perceive us? An interesting exercise can be to ask a family member or friend to provide his perspective of you and then compare his view with your own. Jesus Himself did this when He asked of His disciples, "Who do people say I am?" They answered, "Some say John the Baptist, others say Elijah and still others, one of the prophets." Then Peter responded, "You are the Messiah" (Mark 8:27–29). Jesus replied by affirming Peter's claim.

That's analogous to men today. At some point in time, we had a perception of who we were as individuals, and we continue to seek out a return to that moment when we were whole.

When soldiers return from Iraq, they aren't diagnosed as having "lost their identity," but rather as victims of PTSD, which the National Institute of Mental Health defines as "an anxiety disorder that can develop after exposure to a terrifying event or ordeal in which grave physical harm occurred or was threatened. Traumatic events that may trigger PTSD include violent personal assaults, natural or human-caused disasters, accidents, or military combat."

The recent onslaught of PTSD is a subtle, silent epidemic. Soldiers are returning, many with no visible injuries but scarred nonetheless. The symptoms—which can range from reliving the event over and over, feeling numb to the world, feeling hyper-aroused, feeling angry or irritable, drinking/drug problems, feelings of shame, inability to work or hold a job, relationship problems, abuse, depression, even suicide—may not reveal themselves for days, weeks, or even years. It's a severe and ongoing emotional reaction to extreme psychological trauma.

The main treatment for PTSD is to talk, to share your experience with someone who will not judge or condemn you, someone who will allow you to process what you're thinking and come to terms with the trauma experienced. The more severe cases require medications, but the foundation of any treatment is to have someone whom you can get real with. That's why you need wingmen.

The Purpose of Wingmen

Some men have identified their story and recognized the need for healing, but they think they can go it alone—which is an unwinnable approach. For example, a pornography addict may sense the need to rid himself of the vile habit, but, too ashamed to seek help, he attempts to conquer the addiction on his own. That leads to moments of weakness, where he returns to pornography "just this once" or "only for a few minutes," in order to achieve a short-term buzz. Ironically, he seeks out the very thing that is causing him the most harm. Rather than "just a quick fix," he deepens his shame. It's a vicious cycle that, if not stopped, can drive you to rock bottom, where you're beyond the ability to even ask for help, just when you need it most.

When I was with the Cowboys, Coach Barry Switzer's primary philosophy was that he expected our team to perform on the field and to live up to our end of our contractual agreements. He wasn't there to babysit. We were to arrive on time, practice without complaint, and support each other, without having to be held by the hand or be disciplined.

Of course we had our share of the problems that plague any NFL team—players getting arrested for DUI, drug scandals, promiscuity. At a minimum, these players were seriously distracted from their responsibilities to the team and therefore could not practice or play at the highest level. At a maximum, they endured arrests and suspensions from the team, potentially costing us games—and the difference between success and failure in the NFL is often just a single game. Yet the rest of us never challenged those players by saying something like, "Hey, your behavior isn't just hurting yourself. You're hurting the team."

Yes, those players failed us—but we failed them, too, because we didn't want to take a chance and confront them. We would say to ourselves, "He's a big boy, let him do his own thing." But the right thing would have been to confront these guys as trouble was brewing, because maybe we could have prevented them from slipping and falling. We confront one another not in a rough-handed manner of fronting each other up, but out of care and concern. Galatians 6:1 tells us, "Brethren, if a man is overtaken in any trespass, you who *are* spiritual restore such a one in a spirit of gentleness" (NKJV). The careers of many of these players ended prematurely, due to these issues. Some of them now see the trouble they caused themselves and their team. But we failed them back then, because we did not recognize our own responsibility to demand accountability from those around us. We have to stand up to and for the men on our team and demand from them the same high standards we demand from ourselves.

The same should be true with every man in our society. We should all hold ourselves accountable for our actions, and be trusted to choose between right and wrong. Some men, however, are so buried in their circumstances that they can't help themselves. They're at the depths of their depravity. They're crying out for help even as they make the next bad choice. That's part of the reason that a lot of my former teammates succumbed to the temptations that came with playing for a world champion football team.

Bad choices don't have to be something as awful as committing armed robbery or visiting a prostitute. It could be something as seemingly innocuous as not communicating with your kids, or failing to connect with your wife. It could be not accomplishing the things you want to do, because you don't have the knowledge.

In a multitude of counselors, there's wisdom. As members of the football team, we were strong individuals, but never so strong as we were as a team. With my wingmen at my side, I had the courage and strength to fight through any offensive line. I carried that same strategy off the field when I first formed my men's groups at the ministry.

It's very difficult to make that initial leap of faith and admit that you need help conquering your demons, whatever shape they may take. In Alan Wright's book *Shame Off You*, he discusses how shame is the greatest factor in perpetuating a sin or addiction. By continuing to fail at shaking an addiction, the man feels like an even bigger failure, thus pushing him further down the spiral. By admitting your need to someone safe—someone who will never judge or condemn, even if you slide backward—you take the first step toward healing.

———   — ———

One of the hardest tasks for guys today is breaking down our facade to have a true friendship with another male, a covenantal, David-Jonathan relationship. That is why I created the groups in my ministry. Every other week or so, we meet to lend support to one another. A meeting usually starts with one man offering a testimony up front, whether it's a first-time confessional or his progress in healing. A guest speaker may be brought in to introduce an outside or professional perspective on a recent group topic, or even just to give us guys advice on how to be a better husband, father, businessman, or friend. Sometimes I open up the session myself, to show that I'm in the same fight, and that I need to discuss my troubles and to share my tale with others who might have had a similar experience. My sharing gives the other men permission to open up, to show them that they're in a safe environment where they won't be judged.

Some guys are more comfortable than others with unloading, and smaller groups definitely help make the process more comfortable. For this reason, we break off into smaller groups called elements—units that make up a squadron—which is based upon the military model. The dozen or so men in each element meet every other week. There's no set agenda, just a flexible format for members to give praise reports ("I've been alcohol free for three months.") or to air questions or problems. Between meetings, members communicate via e-mail, phone, or smaller group meet-ups, even calling each other in the small hours of the night when the pressure just gets too great.

These are my wingmen. I use that analogy because these are the men I look to for support and guidance when the road of life gets rocky. Like I mentioned earlier, in the military, if you don't take care of your wingmen and your wingmen don't take care of you, the chances you'll accomplish your mission go way down. The chances also increase exponentially that one of you—if not both—will get shot down or experience another crisis. You have to take care of your wingmen first and foremost.

During the latter part of the Gulf War, my squadron was tasked to be a part of Operation Provide Comfort, whose mission was to defend the Kurdish people fleeing their homes in northern Iraq out of fear that Saddam Hussein would repeat the genocide he committed a couple of years earlier. The U.S. forces went in search of these pockets of refugees to provide military support and drop relief supplies. My initial deployment was from the Royal Air Force station at Bentwaters/Woodbridge in the U.K. to Incirlik, Turkey, a roughly seven-hour flight due to the slowness of our A-10 jets. France granted permission for us to fly through their airspace, but we had to detour around the boot of Italy. Several miles south of the island of Crete, I began experiencing a problem in my number two engine and started to lose oil pressure. Eventually my engine oil pressure showed zero, which according to emergency procedure meant I had to shut down the engine.

There I was, number four in a four-ship of traveling A-10s above the Mediterranean and in dire need of an emergency divert base. Each of my wingmen helped. One read the emergency procedure checklist to confirm I hadn't skipped a step, while another contacted air traffic control in Souda Bay, which had a naval air station. To make matters worse, it was early in the morning on a Greek Easter holiday, so there was minimal staff on duty at air traffic control. We weren't getting vectors, or suggested headings in which to fly, so my wingman helped me navigate while I concentrated on flying the single engine that remained. The A-10 is an underpowered aircraft even with both engines operating, so when you've got only one, there's not much room for error. Add to the situation the fact that we had hot munitions including AIM-9 missiles, and a combat mix of 30 mm bullets on board, and you can understand why this wasn't a training exercise.

But thanks to the support of my wingmen, what could have been a disaster actually ended up being a rather pleasant detour with a bit of R & R included. As we were guided in by the Souda Bay tower, my wingmen followed to ensure I was safe and landed right behind me. We ended up spending a day on the island of

Crete while my engine was repaired, then we headed off to war the following day.

In the Air Force, you train and fight in a two- or four-ship formation, so that you're never alone. You never leave your wingmen. There have been air-combat stories from every major war of the past century in which a pilot had to give up a shot on the enemy because his wingman wasn't there. When he pulled off to take care of his lost wingman, he often found that he would have been shot because the enemy had been right behind!

When Scott Thomas, my football teammate from the Air Force Academy, was a captain in the Gulf War, he lost an engine over the southern part of Iraq and had to eject. All he had on him to defend himself from the Iraqis was a 9 mm pistol. But his wingman stayed overhead and helped coordinate a rescue. The wingman called other aircraft to the site to help keep any potential Iraqis away so that Thomas could get in the clear and eventually get evacuated. Without his wingman, Thomas's final moments could have been at the hands of the enemy.

As Christian men, we face our own enemy: Satan. And Satan is full of ways to tempt us. When it comes to temptation, we must do what Joseph did when Potiphar's wife tried to seduce him: turn and run. You don't even want to mess with temptation. You have to get as far away as possible. And where should you turn? Straight to God and your wingmen, who just might save your life.

Time to Heal

A chaplain friend of mine once told me, "You can't forget something unless you're willing to forgive it." At times we need to forgive ourselves or another individual in order for us to begin to heal our troubled past, even if that past is as recent as a few moments ago. This goes for any trauma, whether it's a child forgiving his abuser or a soldier forgiving the insurgent who shot his friend. Small traumas, such as an argument with a friend or a rear-end fender bender, might cause only a few bruises and some tossing and turning when you're trying to sleep, but the larger traumas might be relived repeatedly, often as night terrors—which are far worse than any nightmare.

In order to relieve these symptoms, we have to forgive so that we can forget. We're able to forgive ourselves the bonehead mistakes we make each day. We have to take that lesson and learn to apply it to bigger issues, both internal and external. We're all fallible, so there's no reason to hold a grudge against someone else because they're not perfect.

I remember one incident from my own life—an incident with a pilot friend of mine. During my first go-round in the Gulf War during Operation Provide Comfort, one of my wingmen and I got in an argument and he said something that really torqued me off. Shortly after our verbal banter, he ended up rotating back stateside and I didn't get to finish the last couple of months in Iraq with him there. After a while, I couldn't even remember what we had argued over. And it always kind of bothered me that we never had a chance to set things right.

A couple of years ago, we ended up having a big reunion with all the old Air Force guys, and this former wingman of mine was there. As soon as I saw him, I went up to him and gave him a big hug. "Man, I don't even know what we were arguing about," I said to him, "but I want you to know that I forgive you." There have been a lot of other times in my life when I've forgiven another person after a disagreement but never been able to actually convey it to them. This time, I got to look the guy in the face and say it. It was great. For the rest of the party, we laughed and carried on, just like the old friends we were.

There isn't always justice in our world. Bad stuff does happen to good people. That's because God blessed us with the gift of free will, and with that comes the possibility of mistakes. In the aftermath of 9/11, for example, people wondered how a loving God could allow such grief and suffering. Christianity teaches that He loves us so much that He gave us the free will to make choices; that if He were a God who dictated our every move in life, we would be automatons.

With free will comes choice. You may not feel it emotionally, but the power is there within you. You may feel powerless over your emotions, but it takes time to learn control over them, such as cravings (most of which are mental, not physical), anger, or fear. Forgiveness is the flip side of anger. Although we may sometimes feel overwhelmed by our tempers, especially when we've been wronged, we need to remember our free will and work toward that place of forgiveness. You may feel that you don't want to forgive people, that they don't deserve it, but you need to work toward it, saying out loud to God that you forgive them. After time, you will find that you feel that forgiveness more and more, and with your forgiveness for another comes healing for you.

The Path to Healing

The key to healing the troubled past is to come to terms with the shameful behavior or guilt and the associated emotion or behavior, and then to invite God in to expunge it. But it's not an overnight fix. Healing the troubled past takes time, possibly years, depending on the severity of your pain and your willingness to forgive. Everybody's unique. Our perception of the world differs based on our experiences. But Christ provides us with commonality, a foundation from which we can all work.

Here's an illustration. After my time in the Air Force, I used to get a lot of mass e-mails from my old flying buddies. As you can imagine, an e-mail from a bunch of former fighter pilots can be pretty explicit—it's not exactly the kind of stuff you'd read to your mom. But sometimes they would also include other stuff, like pictures of a woman in a provocative pose or even soft-core porn. Every time one of these e-mails showed up in our inbox, we guys had to make a choice. So you'd basically sit there and think, "Man, should I?" And you'd end up thinking "Aw, what the heck"—and go ahead and open it. Suddenly it would bring back a flood of old memories from your college days, and you'd be back for a moment in your previous life—and any of the old habits that went with it. Then you'd end up kicking yourself for opening an e-mail you knew you probably shouldn't have opened.

For me, one of my greatest joys in having wingmen was the realization that I had guys I could always unload on. I could share with any one of them something as seemingly harmless as that e-mail. I could call up a buddy and say, "Hey, I had impure thoughts." I no longer had to live in shame. I'd found the strength and freedom to be able to admit to a fellow wingman, "Hey, I screwed up this week. I'm not perfect." I know others in the ministry groups feel the relief, too, because I often hear from members that our meetings are the highlight of their week. This is the kind of thing that makes having relationships with men so crucial, because you can't exactly go up to your wife and say, "Honey, I lusted after another woman today. I gave that second look when I shouldn't have. Forgive me?" Not only is it not going to go over well with her—but you might have to do it twelve to fifteen times a day!

The men in our men's ministry have had a huge impact by being each other's wingmen. Don't get me wrong. We're not a bunch of guys with flowers in our hair, holding hands in a circle and singing "Kumbaya." We're still men who pride ourselves on strength. I look at the ministry groups as a spiritual gym, where we men meet to work out our souls. We would never have the spiritual strength we do if we didn't have our wingmen spotting us and encouraging us on those last ten reps.

If you attended one of our groups, you probably wouldn't notice that it's different from other men's organizations. We talk about hunting and football, and we might even indulge in an occasional adult beverage. (If someone in our group struggles with an alcohol issue, however, we won't burden him, and we'll save the Budweiser or the Shiner Bock for another time.) We meet with our different element groups to discuss common interests. We don't follow a structured, 12-step program; it's about building relationships.

I compare life to a continuous spiritual battle. When you're mired in the depths of a troubled past, you're on the front lines. Mortar shells scream overhead, your position's being bombarded, you're coming under fire. You're in survival mode, reacting without reprieve.

But when you're exposed to light, you begin to pull away from that front line and head to the back for a little R & R—just like the sun-soaked day my Air Force wingmen and I spent in Crete when my engine went out. You're still engaged in the spiritual battle, but you can begin to receive some much-needed attention to your wounds.

The longer you're away from that front line, the more you build up your resistance to the pain. You strengthen your perimeter. But it's still a daily battle. When you first emerge, you're fighting for your life. But as time goes on, it's like rebuilding the wall of Jerusalem as they did in the book of Nehemiah in the Old Testament. You may be rebuilding your section of the wall, but your friends and family have their arms locked around you in protection. Your perimeter is protected by a wingman "warrior" ready to do battle beside you, and a sentry ready to summon support at a moment's notice. Once your section of the wall is fortified, you still can't rest, because there's always a risk of attack. However, with your strengthened perimeter and your comrades-in-arms, it's now easier to defend your position.

> I compare life to a continuous spiritual battle. When you're mired in the depths of a troubled past, you're on the front lines.

CHAPTER THREE

Developing a Work Ethic

When you're part of a farming family, you learn quickly that if you don't work, you don't eat. Since I grew up working the fields on my family's farm in Iowa, developing a work ethic was as important as sowing and reaping the crops each year.

The work was endless. Two thousand head of cattle had to be fed two or three times a day. There were corn and soybeans to plant, tend, and later harvest. Many times, I woke before sunrise to spend the day driving the tractors and trucks. I only took breaks just long enough to eat lunch before we returned to the fields or cattle yard. It wasn't unusual to fall asleep by 8:30 at night, only to be up again at five the next morning. My brother Todd wouldn't have traded the lifestyle for any other in the world.

Because I had a responsibility in the success of our family's farm, I learned about teamwork and commitment at a young age. The work wasn't a burden, I came to realize: it was an opportunity. Working as a family was my first experience with teamwork, long before I set foot on a wrestling mat or football grid.

After a day's work in the fields of baling hay or working with cattle, Todd, who is one and a half years older, would drag me, many times kicking and screaming, to lift weights, throw the football, and work at my overall skill set. Over time, I started to see success—infinitesimal success, but success nonetheless. As I noted my increased speed and strength, I realized how hard work could pay off. My brother planted the seeds of my work ethic, but it was from seeing the fruits of my labor that my self-drive was born.

When I got to high school, I thought I knew what hard work was all about—until I experienced wrestling. It was then I learned that I was really afraid of getting in shape. I experienced my first loss as a freshman because I wasn't in shape. My coach flat out told me, "You are not going to be the wrestler that you want to be until you are willing to pay the price to punish yourself both in the weight room and on the wrestling mat." So I learned about what it took to physically get in shape, but I still lacked the mental toughness that comes with striving to be the best.

I made it to the state tournament my junior year. But I psyched myself out because I didn't know if I had worked as hard as my opponent. In six minutes I was erased from the tournament by a smaller opponent whose work ethic probably exceeded mine. The experience haunted me—and galvanized me. When I returned to training after the season, I gave everything I had, pushing myself even further past my teammates than I had the previous year.

My hard work paid off. This time when I made it to the state championships, I went through the heavyweight division like a knife through butter. When they put the gold medal around my neck in front of fifteen thousand applauding Iowans, I had one thought: "So, this is what you have to do to get here." I'd learned more from losing than I ever had from winning.

Today's society seems to support the belief that it's okay to do the bare minimum—to do just enough to get by. We may not get accolades at work, but at least we won't get fired. We won't be nominated for husband of the year, but at least our wife hasn't divorced us. This mentality of doing the minimum is not the path to success.

In addition to only doing the minimum, we tend to get frustrated and give up if we don't achieve instant results. This is one of the reasons I'm an admirer of Asian culture and philosophy. Here in the United States, if we can't get it done now, within twenty-four hours, we give up. We don't have any stick-to-it-iveness, whereas in Asian cultures, their businesses would have a hundred-year plan. A hundred-year plan would be laughed at in this country where companies are managed for the quarter. In America, if we can't have instantaneous wealth, we believe it's not going to happen. So we just check out. Asian cultures, on the other hand, recognize that important things can take a while to create. Anything in life worth having takes commitment and resolve.

Most men today have never been exposed to the commitment that success requires. If they knew better, they would do better. They see their favorite players scoring touchdowns or slam-dunking baskets, but do they really understand what it took for the athletes to accomplish those goals? A strong, dedicated work ethic went into each of those success stories, and is required for success in any area of your life whether that be family, work, or community. What it takes to develop and maintain the work ethic of a winner is the focus of this chapter.

Take Pride in Your Work

As a teenager, one of my jobs on the farm was what we called "working on the rack." That meant I spent many an afternoon loading baled hay onto wagons under the blazing Iowa sun. All day long I stacked the bales as they emerged from the hay baler, approximately seventy bales to a wagon, each bale weighing as much as seventy pounds.

Then, at the end of my farm workday, I'd meet my high school football and wrestling teammates for a workout in the weight room. Not only did I take pride in my work ethic, but I didn't want to let my teammates down, nor myself. By that point every afternoon, I was exhausted, tired, and sometimes hurting physically, but there was no way I wasn't going to show up for that workout. I had set the goal of being the best that I could be, both on the farm and on the mat—everywhere. That goal would follow me to the Air Force Academy and, later, the NFL.

One of my high school coaches liked to call out guys he thought weren't meeting their potential. "Hey, Chad!" he'd yell. "We've got another room at the high school!" I always took the bait. "What room is that, Coach?" Without fail came the reply: "Room for improvement!"

Whether it was growing up on the farm under my father's supervision or training in athletics, the lesson I always took away was that there are no shortcuts to success. You have to strive toward your goal, and the harder you strive, the greater the pride you can take when you meet your goal. Work hard, and success will come. It may not always be in the form you had envisioned, but good will come of it. Call it a blue-collar mentality, but that's what I was raised to believe.

I went at every task with the will to work harder than anyone else, whether that was in the weight room, in the skies, or on the field. I strove to give it my best and to outwork everybody else. That's what gave me confidence.

To win the state championships, I had to push my way out of an existing comfort zone into a new zone, where, in turn, I'd eventually become comfortable and have to push myself out again. This improvement happened through incremental steps. There's a sweet spot between not doing enough and doing too much, or overtraining. Once you realize you're in that sweet spot, you have to continually adjust and assess whether you are getting better without compromising everything you've achieved so far. In so doing, you'll find your own excellence.

Fellow Iowan and wrestler Dan Gable followed the same set of principles. "Raising your level of performance requires a proper mentality and meaning from within," Gable says. "This gives you the ability and drive to work on the things necessary to go to a higher level. When people ask me how to raise their level of performance, the first thing I ask is, 'How important is it to you?'" It's that level of dedication and determination that won Gable the gold in the 1972 Olympics. Not a single one of his opponents scored a point against him. To this day, he is revered in the world of wrestling.

When I was at the Air Force Academy, we liked to joke among ourselves about "maxing the min" because if the minimum wasn't good enough, it wouldn't be the minimum. Even though we laughed it off, some guys just didn't have the work ethic, so they did the bare minimum to get by. For example, if a physical fitness test (PFT) required thirty-five push-ups in a minute to pass, that's all some of the men would do. They had no pride in themselves or vision of who they were. They would content themselves with a C on their PFT without even trying for the A.

I took a different tack. Throughout my time at the Academy, I prided myself on being one of the first guys in the weight room and one of the last guys out. I wasn't very big—215 pounds at six-foot-four—plus I was slow, only 4.95 for the forty-yard dash. But I consistently put on ten to fifteen pounds in muscle mass and increased my speed each and every year. By the time I was a senior, I had put on two inches and forty pounds, and had cut my time down to 4.68. It took me three and a half years, but my efforts brought me from an undersized tight end to an All-American, Outland Trophy–winning defensive tackle. Was I proud of that trophy? You bet.

The Power of Chair Flying

A fundamental part of work ethic is preparation. If you're not working hard with an eye on the future, you won't be prepared for the events that come your way. As a farm boy, no one had to tell me that preparation could either make or break you. If we didn't sow the crops, we didn't harvest. And if we didn't harvest, we didn't eat.

Probably the best lessons in preparedness I ever received came during pilot training. I knew that becoming a fighter pilot would be tough work, but I never realized just how much until I had actually entered the Air Force. During the first few weeks of the program, we had to absorb more information than I ever thought humanly possible. We had to learn every procedure, every mechanical system before we even flew. Then, with this knowledge loaded in our heads, we had to prove we could call upon it as needed while flying a jet.

We then followed up that training with six to eight months of specialization in the weapons system that we were assigned. Tack on another two years for your first assignment—during which you continue to study your aircraft, aircraft systems, tactics and strategies, your opponent—and you can finally say, after four years, that you're semi-proficient.

Accepting—and embracing—every step of the process helped me realize that developing a solid work ethic is a lifelong process. I learned to content myself with my current sta-

> A fundamental part of work ethic is preparation.

tus, if I knew I had given it my all to get there, but I always then admitted that I had a long way to go to reach my ultimate goal. Training would continue, and I welcomed it, knowing that only by giving it my all would I make it to the next level.

For mental preparation, we often practiced "chair flying," a form of role-playing where we would sit in an ordinary chair that we pretended was a standard cockpit. We would go through different fail scenarios, such as oil system malfunction, or hydraulics failure. We then would go through the motions, pantomiming our actions with our imaginary controls in our imaginary cockpit.

Even once I earned my wings, I continued to chair fly to hone my aviation skills. Doing so gave me confidence in the cockpit, where everything happens so quickly you need to think ten minutes ahead to be able to react in time. Flight training takes years of practice, but by the time you graduate from chair flying to the cockpit, you've already gone through the paces mentally a hundred times. You're ready.

Chair flying shows you the power of the mind and the payoff of patience. You can employ the idea of chair flying in your everyday life by acting out situations before they happen. We've all done this before, whether or not we realized it. Rehearsing a speech or presentation counts, as does stepping into a batting cage for an hour. You're mentally prepping yourself for the real deal.

But not everyone extends this into other areas of their life, such as asking your boss for a raise or imagining how to answer your son when he grows old enough to start asking questions about the birds and the bees. Chair flying these moments before they happen can give you the confidence so that when the time actually does come, it won't seem as difficult as you'd first imagined.

This mental training enables you to make sound decisions and helps you to be proactive rather than reactive, and even to improve your game. There's a story told about a POW in Vietnam who every day would play a round of golf in his mind at different golf courses he had played. When he returned to the States, he had dropped his handicap considerably. This might well be an urban legend, but it sure sounds real to me. What he did, whether he knew it or not, was his own version of chair flying.

Even if you find success, without the foundation of a work ethic, it can be difficult to maintain that level of success. An April 5, 1991, *USA Today* article stated that an NFL survey of 1,000 players showed that 870 had either been divorced, gone broke, or were unemployed six months after the game. That's 87 percent. My guess is that these former players didn't have the foundation to sustain the success they'd worked so hard to obtain—aside from how they identified themselves as nothing but football players. They didn't have the work ethic to sustain them. They stopped chair flying, and as a result, they weren't prepared for the bumps they were about to hit.

I believe we as men should never stop chair flying. Whether that means preparing to fly a jet or lead a business meeting or fight for your marriage, you've got to keep on keepin' on. Readying yourself for the future will lead to far greater prosperity than resting on your laurels while you're ahead, or complaining about your losses while you're down. Part of a work ethic means never giving up. Just visualize what lies ahead. Eventually, you'll get there.

Putting Your Work Ethic to Use in Your Relationships

Work ethic isn't just about tackling the big game or being the best you can be in the athletic or business arena. Developing a work ethic is also crucial to our relationships as human beings. First and foremost, we have to remember that relationships aren't about us as individuals. They're always about the other person or entity, such as your wife in your marriage, the customers in your business, or God Himself. In every relationship in your life, remember this simple truth: it's not about you.

When I flew missions, either in training or in combat, I made a point of seeking to overcome my sense of isolation. I worked at developing a rapport with my wingmen outside of the cockpit—like we talked about in chapter 2. We worked out together, or hit the officers' club at the end of a long day. We talked; we shared. We had to build bonds so that we could trust the same individuals we would be going into battle with. The relationships we forged with one another were based on a core principle: in combat, we had to be willing to give our lives for each other.

In civilian life, it's not often that we're called upon to risk our lives for another human being. But the concept is still the same. In Christian terms, it's what's known as "dying to self." It's giving of yourself to the other person to the point where your own happiness becomes secondary. Any relationship that you value needs to be given this focus—and you must have faith that it's mutual. If the giving and taking are not mutual, then you have to ask yourself if the relationship truly is of value to you. Unfortunately, recognizing an unbalanced relationship is one of the most difficult of life's challenges—second only to acknowledging it. Is there anything worse than the realization that a friend, spouse, or loved one does not care about you as you do for him or her?

But if the feelings and the desire to make the relationship work are mutual, the feeling can be one of elation. And believe me: it doesn't happen overnight. Here's where the "work" part of "work ethic" comes into play. The relationships in your life will only give back to you what you put into them. The going will often be hard, and sometimes it may seem like you'll never make it. Yet if you call upon your well of patience, the rewards will definitely be worth it.

When I talk about developing a work ethic in your relationships, what kinds of relationships am I talking about? *All* of them. It starts with the most basic of God's commandments: "Honor thy father and thy mother." The relationships you build with your parents will last a lifetime—and you'll certainly go through rough spots. I owe much of my work ethic to my father and grandfather, who taught me what it meant to work on a farm and be responsible for my actions. Through my honoring of them, I learned that working hard was a fundamental building block for success.

> The relationships in your life will only give back to you what you put into them.

In the same way that the Bible commands us to honor our parents, we should also show our children respect and expect the same in return. As my wife and I raise our children, we strive daily to show them love and respect. Those relationships take time, too—and more than a small amount of stress and hardship—but I feel incredibly blessed to have them as a part of my life.

My wife and I have certainly gone through our trials, but we've never stopped working on our relationship. Today our marriage is all the stronger for it. I thank God that we didn't throw in the towel when times got tough. And in all of my friendships and even my business relationships, I constantly seek to mirror the same attitudes: love, respect, and a selfless commitment to the other person. I am not the focus of these relationships. By setting my eyes on the other person and *their* needs, I am much better able to grow the relationship in a Godly way.

Your Most Strategic Relationship

The most strategic relationship in our lives as believers is, not surprisingly, our relationship with God. I see many men today confused about God's hand in their lives. For example, in our unstable economic climate, an unemployed worker may hold firm to the belief that God will provide for him. As Psalm 104 states, God provides for the animals, His children—and we as humans fall under that umbrella. So the unemployed worker checks out, waiting for God to deliver. But that's not what the psalm means.

Nowhere is work ethic as important as in our connection to He who created us. Our relationship with God is a strategic one. "A man's heart deviseth his way," reads Proverbs 16:9, "but the LORD directeth his steps" (KJV). In modern parlance, I will call this "noggin navigation." A friend of mine coined this term and I practiced this technique many times with my son on outings when he was young. I would keep a hand on his head, directing him to go here but not there. He was doing the walking; I was only navigating. That's how God works with us. We perform the actions, and God does the guiding.

The belief that God will open all the doors for you is partly true: He will open them, but you must uphold your end of the relationship by looking for them and walking through them. God is not going to carry you through. You must do your share of the work in order to enjoy results. As Benjamin Franklin once said, "God helps those who help themselves."

In Deuteronomy, when the children of Israel left Egypt for the promised land of Canaan, they were continually battling opponents. Before Joshua took over as leader of the Israelites, God told him, "Be strong and of good courage, fear not, nor be afraid of them" (Deut. 31:6 KJV). Sometimes the Israelites faced fierce combat; other times God fought the battle for them, slaying their foes before they even arrived on the battlefield. However, the Israelites never knew beforehand what they would face, but they went anyway, prepared for anything, knowing God was on their side.

Sometimes God blesses us, and sometimes He surprises us. But no matter what we may face, we must hold strong to our beliefs, work toward our goal, and pray that the Lord will bless our steps.

The things I've cherished most in life are the things I've worked hardest for. In all of my achievements, God has been by my side, guiding my next move. He's been cheering me on, monitoring my progress, and spurring me toward greater success. My determination and solid work ethic have provided the fuel for my accomplishments, while God has navigated through them all.

God wants nothing more than to harness your work ethic for His glory. If you give Him that opportunity, you'll unleash the potential within yourself to do all you ever dreamed.

CHAPTER FOUR

Committing to a Balance of Self

God created our world to be in balance. In the United States, our government is unique in that it's a system of checks and balances; the different branches of our government offset one another. A marriage is a balance between the male and female, and God is both masculine and feminine in nature. Balance exists in all parts of life—in the natural order of things, in man-made creations, in politics, in art. The moment we get out of balance, the future starts looking not so good. And when our balance of *self* is off-kilter, we're really headed for trouble.

The "self" to which I refer comprises three parts: body (physical), mind (mental), and soul (spiritual). Physical and mental fitness are the two integral parts of maintaining your self. The spiritual aspect is the glue that holds the whole thing together.

Whether I'm speaking one-on-one with young people or to a thousand-fold audience at a business or church convention, I always talk about the importance of both physical and mental conditioning as a part of my message. Committing to the balance of self, or self-care, involves recognizing the gaps and failings within ourselves, and how these weaknesses may be creating havoc today and catastrophe tomorrow. This means that we need to come to terms with addiction, whether it's socially condoned behaviors like overindulging and overworking or less acceptable vices that we keep hidden, such as those related to alcohol, sex, and drugs.

Caring for yourself is not solely about logging hours at the gym. It's about flexibility, alertness, and mental acuity. It's easy to stereotype a former lineman like me as a jock and nothing more, but I will tell you that I always have my nose buried in a book. I'm always trying to improve my mental edge, not just my physical edge. Leaders are readers. Unfortunately, we live in a society that seems almost profoundly anti-intellectual, where kids are ridiculed if they make a commitment to hitting the books. I think that's tragic. If the scorners only realized how much mental acuity adds to your physical game, we'd have a lot more athletes spending just as much time at the library as they do at the gym.

Committing to self-care on a deeper level means reclaiming our full identities as men, understanding that we are more than our bank accounts, more than our job titles or military rank or the cars we drive. We as men have forgotten our role in society, in our jobs, and in our homes. Self-care means remembering who we are and what we are, so that we can determine what we can truly become.

As we talk about training to be the men we're meant to be,

61

self-care is key. This chapter will discuss the concept of balance in the all-important trinity of your self—body, mind, and soul.

Body Fitness

Since leaving the Cowboys, I've launched a career in the business world in the Dallas area. I so often hear businesspeople say, "I'd love to get in shape, but I don't have the time. I'm working too hard." I don't buy it for a second. You can never work too hard to take care of yourself. In fact if you shift your focus to taking better care of yourself, it will actually help you when it comes to life at work *and* at home.

Your physical fitness translates across the board, from your business relationships to those with your family. On many occasions, I have found that the guys who take care of themselves physically are sharper in negotiations and have more stamina on business trips or when they occasionally have to burn the midnight oil to finish a project. The better physical shape you're in, the more mentally attuned you are, which in turn translates into successful business negotiations and rapport with your family. After a hard day at work, a physically fit man still has the energy to spend time with his wife and kids—and I'm referring to quality time, not sitting in front of the tube watching *The Simpsons* reruns.

> Time should never be an excuse for not being physically fit.

Time should never be an excuse for not being physically fit. Even though we each have only twenty-four hours in a day, those of us who strive for physical fitness will make the choice to find the time. If you decide that watching the latest episode of *LOST* is more important than working on your abs or hitting the treadmill, then that's the choice you've made. Either shut off the TV or get up a half hour earlier. Little, incremental changes will add up in the long run, more so than if you throw yourself into an exhaustive routine that you'll abandon after only a few weeks.

Everybody knows that working out helps you feel and look better. But most men are still not convinced it's worth the time, cost, and trouble. Whether you blame it on laziness, apathy, or indolence, most men can't be bothered to do a single jumping jack let alone commit to a regular workout routine. Unfortunately, they often change their tune once they reach their fifties and discover too late that they have an inflamed prostate or a ridiculously high cholesterol level. Small adjustments over the previous two decades—adding more vegetables to their diet or a daily fifteen-minute walk—could have prevented the twenty or thirty pounds they'd packed on during all their nights on the couch exercising their thumbs on the remote.

If the idea of joining a gym intimidates you, toss it out. You can make these changes at home, lifting light weights or doing a few push-ups first thing in the morning. Simply reducing your alcoholic intake can have huge weight and health benefits, as you'll ingest fewer calories to be worked off. Little changes made consistently over a long period are worth more than a short-lived self-revolution. Beating yourself into submission will only cause you to lose interest, because you'll burn out after just a few tenuous exercise periods. Within three weeks after incorporating a small new habit into your routine, you'll find that maintaining it becomes quite easy, and you'll wonder why you didn't do it sooner. You're then ready to add another small change, and so on.

Don't go it alone. Enlist your wingmen. Doing so will not only help you to set realistic goals, you'll also have a partner with equal stake in your commitment. When you work together as a team, you'll be more likely to stick to your plan, since you're now accountable to another person. You're more likely to get up early to meet at the gym, or leave that last bit of office work for tomorrow to get home in time for your evening walk. It's a mutual affirmation where you're encouraging one another and going through pain together, even if you've each set individual goals. In all my physical endeavors the camaraderie helped me reach my goals more than any coach did. You're more apt to stick to a routine when you have your wingmen than if you're flying solo.

Above all, set realistic goals. Do your research, either by talking with a trainer, reading a book, or searching online, to find a simple, starter workout for your body type. I'm older now than when I played football, so I know not to try to bench-press the whole weight room. I'm fine knowing that there's no way I can run a 4.74 forty. But I'm also not trying to win the Super Bowl—I just want to remain fit. I want to make sure that climbing one flight of stairs doesn't leave me sucking wind. I want to play ball with my kids and not pull a hamstring. Start off with the simple goal of reaching the target zone for your weight, height, and body size. Do that, and you'll be able to play a round of golf without your lower back locking up.

As with the philosophy for the rest of my life, in physical fitness, I concentrate on my core. I do some light free weights, but I mainly concentrate on lighter weights and more repetitions, as opposed to the extremely heavy, low repetitions that I did when I was preparing for football. I don't jog but rather do low-impact aerobics and work on the treadmill or elliptical trainer. My goal is to maintain my body fat the way it is. Studies show that after age forty-five, you lose up to 1 percent of your bone density and muscle mass every year. If you can maintain that same ratio of body fat percentage each year, you're ahead of the game.

Getting and staying fit doesn't require a huge time commitment—twenty to thirty minutes four days a week at a minimum should suffice. But since each person's body and physical condition is different, that time may vary, so consult your physician or a physical fitness professional. Even if you only walk fifteen to twenty minutes at least three days a week and do some light physical weight training twenty to thirty minutes four times a week, you're going to do wonders for your body.

When you think about the time commitment, that amounts to four episodes of *Seinfeld* while you're working out and two albums on your iPod while you're strolling your neighborhood. I think we all can spare that time for the sake of physical fitness. In many cases, you don't even have to sacrifice the activities you would otherwise have been doing. You can combine watching television with working out by downloading it to your iPod or using the gym's television, or you can download books to listen to. I see people reading on exercise bikes and treadmills all the time. So we've just eliminated another excuse as to why you can't find the time!

I have a tip I'd like to share from my training days. When you lift weights, don't do so for more than forty-five minutes, because that's how long your testosterone levels peak at that exercise. If you go beyond forty-five minutes, your testosterone levels drop, so you're getting a diminishing return on your workout. I still never lift more than that, and I usually stay around the thirty-minute range, during which I do high-intensity lifting, which gives me a bit of a cardio workout: high repetitions, lower weight, two to three exercises in a row, with a minute off between. Unless you're planning on becoming a bodybuilder, there's no need to lift weights for two hours at a time.

There are three different ways that you can stimulate the nervous system: changing the number of repetitions, changing the weight, or changing the recovery time between each exercise. When I was lifting weight, by using the Bulgarian method of weight training, I started with three sets of ten repetitions with two minutes' rest between each exercise and worked up to six sets of fifteen with only thirty seconds of rest. For a thirty-minute workout, it was extremely intense, but it helped me go from 275 pounds to 295 and to become the strongest I've ever been. I only changed my routine when my joints started to deteriorate with age.

When working out, the most important area to concentrate on is your core. Everything springs from the core. I've encountered numerous individuals who don't have a strong core, and they all have some sort of physical condition, such as back or neck issues. Strengthening your core will help eradicate many of the conditions most people assume are an unconditional part of aging.

You also have to concentrate on maintaining your flexibility. Very few people I know stretch. They just continue doing the very same workouts as when they were teenagers shaping up for football practice. They don't allow themselves to recover, and they don't warm up or cool down properly. They don't stretch afterward. They static stretch when they should be dynamic stretching.

For those unfamiliar with these terms, static stretching means concentrating on a stationary exercise such as touching your toes while standing in place. A dynamic stretch, on the other hand, incorporates movement with stretching, such as high kicks, which both stretch the leg muscles and provide anaerobic activity. If you've ever watched football players before a game, you've probably seen them doing high-knee bends while pacing ten yards, then turning and doing high kicks. It's a very efficient way of both stretching and warming up your muscles.

In addition to simply looking good, there are more meaningful reasons for maintaining a physical routine and fit condition. You'll gain confidence, be more alert, and increase your mental acuity, to name just a few. But best of all, you'll feel great, years younger than your friends who refuse to give up their couch-potato routine. You need only get up and move to realize what you've been missing out on. Combine physical activity with mental exercises, and you're on your way to feeling like a whole new person.

Mind Fitness

I'm a firm believer that you need to treat your mind like a muscle—if you don't use it, you lose it. It needs to be exercised and stretched to stay in shape. Studies have shown that continuing to do mind-stimulating exercises—simple math problems, reading, Sudoku—keeps your brain agile, just as keeping up a physical routine helps maintain your core strength.

Working out your body and exercising your mind aren't mutually exclusive—physical fitness actually contributes to your mental health. The better the shape you're in, the better your body can process oxygen, which is required for your brain to process at its highest capacity. When you're physically fit, your body is more efficient and processes food at a better rate, allowing your brain the oxygen that it needs.

Too many men don't maintain a mental workout routine after they finish their continuing education. Sure, they may read the newspaper or the latest issue of *Sports Illustrated*, but they never allow their mind to stretch beyond a limited range of subjects. Believe it or not, regular mental exercises—even those as basic as doing the crossword or reading a book on an unfamiliar topic—can help ward off such diseases as Alzheimer's or dementia.

As I've grown older, I've become more philosophical, which is partly due to the fact that I'm now reading twice as many books as I did when I was in my thirties. I find it fascinat-

> Treat your mind like a muscle—if you don't use it, you lose it.

ing that I've acquired such a profound love of books at this point in my life. Broadening the different genres I read has helped me translate newly acquired information into my daily life, such as in business conversations or understanding why individuals behave the way they do.

One of the most important areas of information I've accumulated through my years of reading has been in human behavior. I have a better grasp of why people from certain cultures or demographics behave a certain way, and I've used that knowledge to facilitate in business or other venues. Having such information allows me either to empathize or to develop a solution based on commonalities from our differing backgrounds.

Even in friendships I've found that coming from a deeper understanding is always useful. Rather than become frustrated in a situation, I've been able to approach the problem with some of my friends' experiences in mind, which has allowed me to glimpse the facts through their eyes. Having such knowledge has prevented many an argument, and I'm sure it's saved more than one friendship. People's perceptions, their experiences, and their histories are their reality. I try and get a feel as to where a person is coming from before I even say a word or help in offering any advice or solutions.

Just as with your physical routine, you have to find a balance in your life to make room for your mental workout routine. You can even combine the two to save more time, such as reading while you're on the treadmill or listening to a book on tape while lifting weights. When you look at your list of priorities and see that your family and reading fall way above SportsCenter, it will be easier to make the decision to read to your kids at night instead of flopping down on the couch with a remote. My wife and I regularly share books that we think the other will enjoy, which helps strengthen the bond between us, just as it does when I share a book with friends. We develop a deeper camaraderie by discussing the book later on, whether or not we both like it or agree on its viewpoints.

Mix it up. Read books that inspire you toward positive action, but don't get in a rut. Try adding some biographies, history, and classic or contemporary fiction. Think of a diverse reading list as cross training for the brain. And don't limit yourself to reading alone—you have to stimulate yourself with different exercises and goals, such as improving your vocabulary, finishing crosswords, or even playing Trivial Pursuit with your family. You're keeping things fresh by mixing up your routine, just as you would rotate machines at the gym.

We want our kids to do more than just perform well in an individual sport, right? We want to prepare them for a lifetime of physical fitness. The same is true for intellectual pursuits. My wife and I work constantly to instill an understanding for both physical and mental fitness in our children. We're fortunate that our kids' school promotes a love of reading—especially the classics—because reading and appreciation for literature needs to be taught, just as my brother's dragging me to the weight room helped instill a work ethic in me. We have to be the example.

And just in case you're uncertain about taking intellectual instruction from an athlete, let me share a story with you. Once I was being interviewed by a reporter from *Sports Illustrated*, who told me, "Man, you don't have the vocabulary of a typical NFL football player, particularly a lineman." I had to laugh. Of course I reminded him that, before I was a lineman in the NFL, I had a "real job" as an Air Force fighter pilot where I was constantly engaged in mental gymnastics. And ever since, I've done my best to keep my brain as active as my body.

But I'm by no means an isolated case. I know so many professional athletes who are nothing like the stereotypical meatheads—they're intelligent and well-spoken individuals who keep themselves in top mental shape, too. What have these guys figured out how to sustain? A dynamic balance of self, meaning a mastery over both mind and body.

Soul Fitness

Maintaining your mental and physical fitness requires a lot of discipline. The two work in tandem, so that commitment to one area will bring about riches in the other, and vice versa. But what fuels your progress in these two areas of your life? What governs your body and mind fitness?

The answer is simple: your spirit.

I saved the discussion of our soul fitness until the end, because it's undoubtedly the most important. The third piece of the puzzle—your spiritual balance—helps you master the other two aspects of your self. It's at the core of what it means to be a strong Christian man.

The connection between your physical, mental, and spiritual sense of balance is not always apparent. Think of it this way:

your spiritual fitness is like the roof of a great temple. It presides over the mental and physical pillars with overarching authority and magnificence, and all three components are vital to the building's glory and purpose. But if you begin to cut corners in the physical and mental areas of your life, the roof of that temple—your spiritual self—begins to slip a little to the side as the pillars start to crumble. In other words, when you start to slack off on your commitments to your mind and body, it's easier for you to rationalize doing so elsewhere, such as in your relationships or your morals.

The story of David and Bathsheba illustrates this concept. When David became tempted by looking at Bathsheba, what was he doing? He certainly wasn't exercising discipline, since he wasn't with his troops in battle where he should have been. The Bible says that David was hanging out in his palace during the season when kings were to be in the fields with their armies. Instead, he had rationalized why he should be in his palace rather than performing his kingly duty on the battlefield, which led to his laying eyes on a beautiful woman bathing at dusk.

Although David knew the woman to be Bathsheba, the wife of one of his mighty men, Uriah, he lay with her and she conceived a child. In order to conceal the identity of the father, David tried in vain to get Uriah to leave battle and visit his wife, so that he might think himself the father. But, unlike David, Uriah refused to take the pleasure of being with his wife when his troops and fellow soldiers were in the field of battle. At David's orders, Uriah was left to die on the battlefield, and David married Bathsheba.

The Lord was so displeased with David's actions that He allowed David and Bathsheba's son to die. This act, as well as David's lack of fatherly oversight, set a bad example for his sons who engaged in similar activities, thus starting the downward spiral of Israel's kings. Had David not strayed from the righteous path and been with his troops, he would not have been tempted by Bathsheba and felt the wrath of the Lord.

David lost a part of himself when he gave into temptation, when he abandoned his men in battle and slept with his loyal soldier's wife. For a non-military man who has not experienced the horrors of war, the loss of identity equates to losing a part of yourself or what God meant for you to be. This may be due to activities we have done, or things we have no control over. But the moment we lose a sense of balance, we are in grave peril of forfeiting the rich future God has in store for us.

Christ has paid the price for you through His sacrifice on the cross. And if you confess by your mouth that Jesus is Lord and believe that God raised Him from the dead, your salvation is secure. But just because we experience God's grace doesn't mean we don't need to exercise discipline. Balance does not occur on its own—you have to discipline yourself in order to create it. Saint Paul spoke of the spiritual reigning over the physical and mental to discipline ourselves. We were given our minds and bodies as a grant, not a gift. It is our responsibility and duty to take care of them. Our body and mind are not in control. It's our spirit.

> Our body and mind are not in control. It's our spirit.

———·———

God is one God and three persons, the Father, the Son, and the Holy Spirit. A human being is also one individual with three parts, the physical body, the mind, and the spirit. Keeping your identity in focus helps maintain the balance of the trinity of your self. When we allow the balance of the three to get out of whack, we're in trouble.

Perhaps you've compromised your balance by allowing addictions to take over or by letting yourself become physically unfit. That's when it's important to regain your balance by praying for forgiveness and for your spirit to be rejuvenated, for the Holy Spirit to fill you with strength and power. By getting back on track spiritually, you can then begin to control the physical and mental areas of your life.

We've talked about crafting your vision to be a man of God. Committing to self-care is a part of the overall vision: it's the foundation on which everything else is built. First you must commit to achieving spiritual balance by establishing your identity in Him. You need to define and affirm who you are—to believe what God says about you and His specific purpose for you. Once that's done, the other pieces—the physical and mental—fall into place.

In the next few chapters, we'll talk in more depth about finding fulfillment and living your spirituality. Because only by achieving that balance and keeping our identity in strong focus are we able to determine what we can truly become.

CHAPTER FIVE

Finding Fulfillment

When's the last time you browsed the self-help section at your local bookstore? It's a far cry from a solitary row or two—there are endless shelves of books by people who guarantee they've got all the answers. Whether you're struggling through relationship issues, low self-esteem, money crises, or addiction, these books promise to fix your pain. According to a recent survey, the "self-improvement" market in 2008 net well over $11 billion in the U.S. alone. Why have we as a culture become so obsessed with "fixing" ourselves?

The answer is easy: because people are searching for meaning. The self-help industry is thriving because, in their quest for fulfillment, the masses will search anywhere, even if the solution is temporary—a spiritual Band-Aid. But the reason these self-help organizations cannot help you find fulfillment is that they internalize the process. They preach that by thinking positively and meditating on your success, fulfillment will come to you.

I'm here to tell you that it just isn't so. Success is not an endgame. Success is a by-product of defining who you are as an individual and finding the meaning in your life. And that meaning is either doing a deed or work, or doing something for someone else. It's not found within you.

Some contemporary self-help systems have their foundations—whether they know it or not—in the Bible. Work, goal-setting, teamwork—all are Biblical principles. I believe many people of Christian faith have lost track of this truth and have turned to these organizations who can translate only a small fraction of the truth of the Bible. Their version is a diluted truth that becomes how you define yourself as an individual. You're led to believe that your mind can influence your existential surroundings, that through positive thoughts you can manipulate your destiny. That's as far from the truth as you can get.

Finding fulfillment equals developing meaningful, rewarding commitments. A person must ask him- or herself, "What exactly am I committed to?" The answer could be the relationship with your spouse, friends, family, community, or God. In my case, my purpose is to help others find their purpose.

We live in what has been called a "microwave society," where we feel entitled to instantaneous gratification. Our greatest ethos seems to be, "Let nothing interfere with my pursuit of pleasure." I see this today with college students who, immediately upon graduation, expect the lifestyle their parents built over forty years. I see it in football, with a second-round draft choice who believes that his $1.2 million signing bonus entitles him to a starting position and the respect that his seasoned team members have had to earn. Fulfillment doesn't come in an instant. You can't cook it up in a microwave, but that's what society is telling our kids—and us, too.

I'm saying something very different. Fulfillment is, quite simply, commitment to a meaningful goal: your life's purpose.

If the goal you choose is indeed meaningful, it won't change drastically over time. Your purpose will stay pretty much the same from the moment you set your sights on the target. Understanding this can help you move past the microwave mentality and realize that true goals aren't those you reach in six months, but rather the ones that you're still working on a lifetime from now. When you seek instant gratification, you're more likely to compromise your integrity by cutting corners to achieve your goal in the time you see as reasonable, not what is truly plausible. But if you have a strong foundation as to who you are as an individual, you'll be less likely to make such compromises, because you'll have a better understanding of how they'll affect the rest of your life.

In this chapter, we'll discuss how fulfillment comes from the pursuit of worthy goals. Finding fulfillment is all about the process; it has nothing to do with the fleeting feelings of satisfaction we all experience from time to time. True fulfillment is much deeper and far more profound. First of all, it requires understanding the unique "Why" of your life.

Understanding the Why

The crux of fulfillment comes down to the aspect of why: Why do we do what we do? What propels us in our everyday actions? Why do we go to work? Why do we work out? Why do we read books? We as humans want to know why we're here, the meaning behind our lives. We all want to know the answer to one question: Why?

I want to debunk the myth that it's impossible to reach fulfillment in your life. To do so, I'd like to turn to two great thinkers from history—a philosopher and a psychologist. And to the Bible, of course!

Blaise Pascal, the renowned French philosopher to whom mathematicians are forever indebted for Pascal's triangle, said:

> What else does this craving, and this helplessness,
> proclaim but that there was once in man a true happiness,
> of which all that now remains is the empty print and trace?
> This he tries in vain to fill with everything around him,
> seeking in things that are not there the help he cannot find
> in those that are, though none can help, since this infinite
> abyss can be filled only with an infinite and immutable
> object; in other words by God himself. (*Pensées* [New York:
> Penguin Classics, 1995], 45)

On the cusp of the European Enlightenment when many philosophers would abandon God altogether for reason, Pascal declared that man's search for significance is a huge vacuum that can be filled only by God.

This doesn't mean that our individual identity is without purpose. Though we are each filled with a God-shaped vacuum, our life derives meaning from our identity: the unique skills and talents God has bestowed upon us. Finding fulfillment is finding the meaning of who you are *in Him*.

The Viennese psychiatrist Viktor Frankl, founder of the existential analysis known as logotherapy, said:

What man actually needs is not a tensionless state, but rather the striving and struggling for a worthwhile goal, a freely chosen task... Everyone has his own specific vocation or mission in life to carry out, a concrete assignment which demands fulfillment. Therein he cannot be replaced nor can his life be repeated. Thus, everyone's task is as unique as is his specific opportunity to implement it. (*Man's Search for Meaning* [Boston: Beacon Press, 2000], 110, 113)

Frankl is saying that we are all special. We each have a chosen task in this world to fulfill. When God made each and every one of us unique, He gave us specific tasks and abilities to perform our life's work.

Frankl was, in fact, paraphrasing the Parable of the Talents. In the book of Matthew, a master divided his property into units called "talents" and gave the talents to his three servants according to their ability. He gave one servant five talents, another two talents, and the final one he gave one talent. After some time, the master returned to find that both the five-talent servant and two-talent servant had doubled their money, while the one-talent servant did nothing. As punishment, the master took the one talent the servant had and gave it to the one who had ten talents.

The moral of the story is that although we are not created equal, we are all created unique, with unique talents that we must learn to use to the best of our abilities. We then use those talents to pursue our purpose, our why, our meaning as to who we are.

Frankl himself is a perfect example of this belief. His story is truly extraordinary and inspirational. He had everything taken away from him—his material possessions, his family, even his identity—when he was thrown into a concentration camp. Yet, in spite of the most formidable of circumstances, he would not allow his focus to waver. He made it a point to serve his fellow prisoners by helping them find a will to live, a reason to continue despite the bleakness of their situations. Being imprisoned couldn't take away his spirit. It was in this most depressing and soul-crushing of environments that Frankl formulated his theory that, no matter what our surroundings or circumstances, life can have meaning. He became living proof of Nietzsche's saying: "He who has a why to live for can bear almost any how."

"One of the unique features of human existence," Frankl affirms, "is the capacity to rise above certain conditions, to grow beyond them. Man is capable of changing the world for the better, if possible. And of changing himself for the better, if necessary." He goes on to say:

> There is a danger inherent in the teaching of man's
> "nothingbutness," the theory that man is nothing but
> the result of biological, psychological, and sociological
> conditions, or the product of heredity and environment.
> Such a view of man makes a neurotic believe what he is
> prone to believe anyway, namely, that he is the pawn and
> victim of outer influences or inner circumstances. This
> neurotic fatalism is fostered and strengthened by a psy-
> chotherapy which denies that man is free. (*Man's Search
> for Meaning* [Boston: Beacon Press, 2000]; 130)

Frankl's beliefs conflict with the current trend in society, which tends to say that we don't need to take accountability for who we are. But Frankl

> Only by taking ownership of *who* we are will we be able to discover the truth of *why* we are.

had it right, and our society has it wrong. Only by taking ownership of *who* we are will we be able to discover the truth of *why* we are.

Viktor Frankl was able to find fulfillment, even amid the soul-crushing environment of a concentration camp. The bottom line is: your circumstances don't matter. You have in you the inherent ability to seek God's purpose each and every day of your life. God gave us free will, so the choice is yours. The only obstacle to seeking and finding fulfillment is you.

Defining Your Purpose

My all-time favorite movie is a John Wayne film called *The Searchers*. The premise is that John Wayne is coming back to live with his brother and his family after having served three years in the Civil War. Upon returning home, he faces a raid by a band of Comanche Indians, who murder his brother, his sister-in-law, their son, and one of their daughters, and abduct the other daughter. John Wayne goes on a long journey for several years, trying to find this Indian band to rescue his niece. By the movie's close, he is totally engaged with this journey, this task. He's become hardened, bitter, conniving, and when he does find the girl—who is now a young woman—he'll try to kill her because she has been soiled by the world.

John Wayne, of course, kills the bad guys, does indeed rescue the girl, and brings her home to a new family. The young man who had accompanied him on his journey goes off with his fiancée, and all the other people in the story go back to their spouses or rejoin their families. All in all, everything works out...for everyone else.

At the very end of the movie, John Wayne's character is watching everyone else walk into the door of their home. He's standing there at the doorway. Does he go in? No, of course not. He's a lone figure in the world, the archetypal John Wayne character. He didn't have a relationship to be a part of, and he's seen sulking in his sorrows. So what does he do? He turns around and he walks away.

It's a phenomenal ending to an amazing movie, but it's not exactly my idea of the way a man should live his life.

I truly believe that we were not meant to "John Wayne" it through life, to wall ourselves off from love and connection. We have to know who we are, and we have to know what we stand for, but we cannot stand for that shut-down, emotionally unavailable warrior that John Wayne often played in his films.

What I take from that movie is the fact that when you spend your whole life working—busting your butt for your family—you help them achieve their goals, like financial stability and a roof over their heads. But, like John Wayne in the movie, you can be so consumed with working that you neglect the ones you're working for. At some point you wake up and realize that you are so focused on the task at hand that you missed out on the relationships, the blessings that life provides.

All too often, men are so focused on their mission, like John Wayne in *The Searchers*, that they miss out on their kids growing up. They miss out on their relationships with their wives and all the joy God had for them, because they were so consumed with the task of earning money and creating a good standard of living for the family. When all is said and done, they've missed out on the true meaning of fulfillment.

This is where a man has to realize that his purpose in life is not strictly material. In fact, it has nothing to do with that. Your purpose, the individual "who" of the man you are, primarily wraps around your relationship with God.

Imagine that you're on your deathbed right now. Looking back on your life, you can see you were financially successful. You made a lot of money, lived in a large home, and always drove the newest-model car. You owned your own company, which was tops in its field, and were viewed as an unrivaled businessman not to be messed with.

But your kids, whom you hardly know, don't even like you. They have no interest in carrying on the business legacy you slaved to create. Your wife left you long ago, having grown tired of coming second to your work. In the final moments of your life, you find yourself utterly alone.

At that moment, what would you say your life's purpose has been? It wasn't family, and it certainly wasn't charity. Your purpose has been work, pure and simple. Your "why" has been chasing the next buck, getting the next promotion, and taking over your rival business. In your pursuit of fulfillment, you failed to see that you were never filling the void in your life. By searching for a purpose outside of yourself, you were actually making that void larger. An external purpose can be taken away. And if it's taken away, your purpose as an individual is gone.

It's not uncommon to hear of a successful businessman who, after forty years of work, dies within a few years of retiring. He's lost his purpose, because he chose to seek fulfillment externally. Materialism is not a goal.

Many times we set our goals so far into the future that we don't take advantage of the joy, love, and beauty in the here and now. We get so wrapped up in the Endgame that we miss out on the journey. Like John Wayne, we walk back into our comfort zone—whether it's workaholism, isolation, or bitterness—and we miss out on the good stuff. That's where having meaning helps. Since a truly meaningful goal has no end, you can be content no matter where you are on life's path. Having a true purpose in life means never seeing that purpose completely filled. It's a project that requires constant attention, but in return reaps constant spiritual rewards. Your goal must be all-encompassing.

When you "walk with God," you come to the realization that at every moment of your day, you are leaning on Him, relying on Him, performing your duties for Him. The work never ends. It's all day long. But throughout it all, He is beside you. Either God is everything, or God is nothing. You can't take a middle-of-the-road attitude. You're either all in, or you're not.

Think about it from a practical standpoint. We're still in Basic Training, right? If your first and foremost goal is to be victorious, take a moment to consider how you define victory. I would equate "victory" with "survival"! There are people who actually enjoy Basic Training—and frankly, they scared me back in the day when I went through it! The main thing is to survive the physical and psychological ordeal that Basic Training represents. If your goal in Basic Training is to lead troops into battle, win wars, and save democracy, you're getting a little ahead of yourself. There will be time for all those important things. For now, what you really want to do in Basic...is just live to tell the tale.

It's the same with your life strategy. Define what it would mean to you to win in life. Perhaps it's being happily married until the end of your days. Or maybe it's watching your kids grow up to be happy, independent adults with whom you share a close bond. Maybe it's being well respected in the community, at your job, or in your congregation.

How do you go about accomplishing any of these goals? Go back to chapter 3: develop your work ethic, and commit to it. Work hard and put in the time. Take your children as an example. You need to spend quality time with them to establish a bond. Talk to them, and let them know they can always talk to you. Discipline them, but let them know that you do it because you love them. And tell them you love them every day.

Will you have to put other commitments on the back burner to put your kids first? Sacrifice your time and energy? Miss business meetings? Spend a camping trip sleeping on the hard ground in a pup tent when you want nothing more than to sink into your Memory Foam mattress at home? Probably yes to all of the above. Just remember the term "dying to self." It means giving up yourself for the betterment of the ones you love.

Keep Your Eyes on Your Purpose

The path to finding your life's purpose involves trial and error, and it may very well send you in different directions all at once. This can be frustrating and confusing, not to mention exhausting, in a world where our schedules are already jam-packed. When pursuing your life's purpose, how do you keep your eyes on the goal?

I had to learn the hard way that I can't be all things to all people. I took on too many responsibilities, because I saw them all as worthy causes—fund-raising events, charities, faith-based organizations. But even though each had its own positive merits, these causes eroded my own sense of fulfillment. Not all of them coincided with my purpose, and so instead detracted from it. Although I was doing the right thing for these worthy organizations, it wasn't the right thing for me, because it detracted from my purpose of serving my family.

Today I've centered on my purpose by aligning myself with a handful of charitable organizations, the ones I found to be most in line with my sense of purpose and thus providing me the greatest sense of fulfillment. This reorganization of priorities has allowed me, in return, to give them the attention they each deserve, while at the same time letting me focus on the most important people in my life.

Keep your eye on the prize. Know your talent and your purpose and stay focused. You do not need to be all things to all people. Stretching yourself thin will only endanger your sense of fulfillment, which will keep you from helping these entities. Keeping your eyes on your true purpose will help not only you but also the people or organizations at the center of your life's purpose. If it doesn't agree with your life's purpose, then don't do it. It's that simple.

Each of us was created to seek fulfillment by taking part in something bigger and greater than ourselves. Frankl said we could do this in one of three ways: by creating a work or doing a deed, by experiencing something or encountering someone, or by the attitude we take toward unavoidable suffering.

If you find yourself losing track of your purpose, try the following exercise, which my wife and I try to do. Think about who you are, not who you perceive yourself to be. Explain an area of your life and what you're doing. For example, you might be holding a seminar at your church to provide advice on running small businesses. Then ask your spouse or friend what they see, how they perceive you in this aspect. Perhaps they see your time commitment as self-serving, a marketing plan in the guise of community involvement. Ask yourself if this is indeed the case and, if not, what would lead them to this conclusion. In some cases, your perception is reality. But sometimes how others perceive you may differ from how you perceive yourself. Honest feedback can help you in meeting your goals.

You don't need to be financially wealthy to find a meaningful purpose. I've had teammates who played in the NFL longer than the 3.5-year average, only to emerge broke a year later. Some very well-to-do individuals I know are also some of the most miserable people I know. None of these people are happy, or even content. Their money can't alleviate the pain of not knowing their kids or of divorcing their wives.

Some tribes, such as those in the Amazon or Southeast Asia,

live a subsistence lifestyle—and could be rated as being happier than most Western people. They have food, shelter, and, above all, family. When materialistic values—derived from the negative view of our culture—are introduced, however, their society goes into a state of upheaval. In China, for example, parents leave their children with their grandparents for upwards of a year while they go in search of a better living. They chase a fleeting materialistic dream anchored in money, but realize too late that they have missed out on their child's life. They've forgotten the priorities that have sustained their culture for centuries and replaced them with empty, money-oriented goals.

The ultimate answer to "Why?" is that each of us is here to serve God, and we do that by caring for each other. Finding our purpose means going on the journey of discovering exactly how we fit into God's master plan. And it is an incredible journey—one that takes a lifetime, but promises the sweet fruits of fulfillment all along the way.

> The ultimate answer to "Why?" is that each of us is here to serve God, and we do that by caring for each other.

CHAPTER SIX

Living Your Spirituality

Our society is full of role models. The only problem is there are just as many bad ones as good ones. Let's take sports as an example. It's hard to think of a sport in today's world that generates a lot of admiration and trust. Baseball players? On the juice. If it isn't steroids, it's HGH, which is still undetectable but offers many of the same benefits as steroids. Basketball players? The NBA today, by and large, symbolizes selfish play and a quest for putting up numbers for contract time instead of a commitment to winning. And the private lives of many NBA players, from gunplay to having children with a number of different women, is hardly something we would hold up as an ideal for young people.

Even my sport, football, is not immune. Recently, Patriots coach Bill Belichick has been called "Coach Belicheat" for his role in a signals-stealing controversy that cost him and his organization a $750,000 fine and a first-round draft choice. And while most of the NFL players I've known over the years have been very fine individuals, they're not the ones who receive the headlines. It practically takes a law degree to read through the jurisprudence section of the sports page, just to be able to figure out who's on trial for what off-the-field crime or act of mayhem.

The business world takes its lumps, and nobody needs to recount one more time the events at Enron, WorldCom, Global Crossing, Adelphia, or Tyco. Government, often enmeshed with business, is the same way—let's not forget the lack of oversight with Wall Street, Fannie Mae, and Freddie Mac that plunged the nation—and the world—into economic turmoil. The real problem is that the business climate today sends the following message to businesspeople and to young people entering the business world: it's only cheating if you get caught. It's possible to find businesspeople who serve as positive role models for young men and women, but unfortunately, it takes some real looking to track them down.

Our church leaders are not the ultimate role models, either. The news is frequently filled with stories of lapsed pastors struggling with sex addiction, homosexuality, and other temptations of the flesh. Unfortunately, when a Christian leader stumbles, our faith often stumbles as well, because we have put so much energy and faith and trust in him. We think to ourselves, if this great, mighty man of God stumbles, what does that mean for me?

If we look to human beings as role models, we're always going to be disappointed. That's because there's only one true role model: Christ. He was fully man when He came down to Earth, and He had every temptation thrown at Him across the board, from money to power. Yet He was able to withstand all of those and live an exemplary life. Unlike our Christian leaders who all have faults and weaknesses, Christ has never let us down. When we're looking for guidance as to how to lead our lives, Jesus Christ is the ultimate role model.

Striving to be like Christ is at the core of living our spirituality as Christian men. Of course that doesn't mean that we're going to be successful at it. We can bust our butts all day long trying to be as much like Christ as possible, but we're never going to hit it. We're all going to sin, because man is fallible. One of my friends sums it up like this, "Try not to sin, *BUT when you do*, pick yourself up and confess to God. 'My sin is not me; it's not what You created me to be. I don't want to continue this. Forgive me.'" Then you keep on going. You keep pressing on, trying to emulate Christ in all the different parts of your life.

So how do we do it? From a practical standpoint, how do we strive to be like Christ in our daily lives? In this chapter, we're going to talk about living your spirituality. It all starts with suiting up. A soldier's first move is to dress for battle, just like a football player's first move is to don his uniform before a game. And when it comes to living your spirituality that means clothing yourself in the Armor of God.

Once you've done that, it's time to get your hands dirty with a little wrestling. Living your spirituality means accepting that there will be times when your faith is tested, and there will be times when you wrestle with failure. There will even be times when you wrestle with God. I'm here to tell you from personal experience: that's okay. In fact this kind of wrestling is all a part of God's plan. It's all a part of Basic Training to get you ready for active duty the rest of your life.

The Armor of God

The first part of striving to be like Christ is learning how to fight off temptation. Christ was tempted by Satan several times, and he never faltered—an unbeatable record. As humans and sinners, we can't hope to achieve the same success rate. But if we clothe ourselves in the Armor of God, we'll be far better equipped to deal with temptation when it presents itself.

The book of Ephesians paints a vivid picture of the Armor of God. And if you think about it, it's a pretty good analogy. Every day we wake up as Christians, we have to arm ourselves for battle: the battle of living our spirituality as Christian men and facing a world of temptations. Lucky for us, the Bible gives us a whole tool chest of equipment designed to help us do just that. Ephesians 6 says:

> Finally, my brethren, be strong in the Lord and in the power of His might. Put on the whole armor of God, that you may be able to stand against the wiles of the devil. For we do not wrestle against flesh and blood, but against principalities, against powers, against the rulers of the darkness of this age, against spiritual *hosts* of wickedness in the heavenly *places*. Therefore take up the whole armor of God, that you may be able to withstand in the evil day, and having done all, to stand. Stand therefore, having girded your waist with truth, having put on the breastplate of righteousness, and having shod your feet with the preparation of the gospel of peace; above all,

taking the shield of faith with which you will be able to quench all the fiery darts of the wicked one. And take the helmet of salvation, and the sword of the Spirit, which is the word of God; praying always with all prayer and supplication in the Spirit, being watchful to this end with all perseverance and supplication for all the saints. (Eph. 6:10-18 NKJV)

When I speak about the Armor of God, I also compare it to football equipment. If I'm giving a presentation to kids, I get out my football uniform and use it as a visual aid. At "having girded your waist with truth," I point to the belt around my football pants—the Belt of Truth—that stands for character and how to define truth. The Breastplate of Righteousness is the shoulder pads. It protects the heart, where Christ lives. The feet with the readiness that comes from the Gospel of Peace—those are your cleats. They protect those who spread His gospel, and who take the risk of sharing. The Shield of Faith is the elbow pads. We use them to protect against the blows of a blocker, to protect us against the blows we take in life, whether they be adversity, sickness, death, or disappointment.

The Helmet of Salvation is obviously the football helmet. What does a helmet do? It protects our head. So, what is the Helmet of Salvation? It protects us during the battle of ideas for our mind in today's "New Age" relativistic environment. You may encounter ideas in a college course, for example, or in the workplace that define success as being "things of this world." How do you defend or represent your faith in today's culture?

That's the battle of ideas. And you've got to be hard-headed about what you know to be true—which is where the Helmet of Salvation comes in handy.

So we've got the Belt of Truth, the Breastplate of Righteousness, the Shield of Faith, the Helmet of Salvation, and our feet are shod with the readiness that comes from the Gospel of Peace. There's only one item left: the Sword of the Spirit.

The Sword of the Spirit is the only offensive weapon mentioned in the Bible. The other tools are all defensive weapons that protect you against the world and what Satan throws at you. But God does not intend for us to be passive as Christian men. So He has given us a tool to fight back against the onslaught of sin.

I liken the Sword of the Spirit to the football. This football, this offensive weapon, is God's word. It's the only offensive weapon we have, and it's going downfield to score points. In our spiritual lives, we can go on the offensive by reading His word and studying the scriptures, by attending Bible studies, and by praying. At all times, we can rest assured in the knowledge that we are already victorious. Christ has won our ultimate battle for us.

———

Pray continuously. That's how we communicate our desires to God, and how He can communicate through us. Prayer is the game plan. On the football field, you've got coaches on the sidelines and coaches up in the press box. They're involved in everything; they're looking at what the opposing team is doing and how they're maneuvering. From your position on the field of play, you can't know what they're doing in their backfield, or see how they're maneuvering, or process what plays they are running over a period of time. Sometimes we want to call our own plays, but when we call our own plays on the field, we don't have the benefit or the wisdom that comes from having multiple coaches who can see everything.

On the field of life, we need to be even more mature and wise. The way we do this is through prayer. Prayer is how the coach on the sidelines—in this instance, God—gets the play on the field for the quarterback. If we're tuned in to what our coach is telling us, we can use our offensive weapons—His word, His Scripture—or our defensive weapons to maneuver the tactics and strategy on the field. That way we never deviate from God's game plan for our lives.

When most people read the passage in Scripture describing the Armor of God, they can't picture what is being described because Paul wrote it as an analogy of a Roman soldier dressed for war: the battle garments, the sash belt, the sword, and the sandals. But everybody knows what a football player looks like. That's why the analogy of the Armor of God to a football uniform works so well. When I talk to children, I usually get the smallest individual there, male or female, and go through each one of these things, putting on the pieces as I talk. I'll dress them in my helmet and shoulder pads, then the jersey and my big cleats. At the end, they carry the football. It looks ridiculous, but they'll always remember the impression it makes.

Once you're clothed in the Armor of God, you're ready for whatever circumstances may be thrown your way. You're also ready to get out on the mat and wrestle with a partner you may not have been expecting—a partner named God.

Wrestling with God

I meet an awful lot of people who are under the impression that as Christians, they are entitled to a "get out of jail free" card. They believe that if you're a Christian, you will never experience any type of trouble such as sickness, death, bankruptcy, acts of violence, or whatever else one might come up against. A lot of times, when people start a new endeavor and immediately hit resistance, they think "God is against me!" and decide "I'm not going to do this." It even happens in personal relationships. A newly married couple has their first quarrel and one of them thinks, "Well, maybe I wasn't supposed to get married" or "This was supposed to be easy!"

The truth is, you don't really know the strength of your faith until it's been tested. In 1 Corinthians 16:9, Saint Paul says, "A great door for effective work has opened to me, and there are many who oppose me." What an amazing attitude to take. Instead of focusing on the opposition, Paul focuses on the door. He's looking at the ability to do great work, even in light of the adversity, obstacles, and resistance he knows he'll have to face.

God tests your faith, your strength, and your character. Faith, just like any type of aircraft, needs resistance. In order for it to take off and soar, it has to take off into the wind. Part of living your spirituality means accepting that God is in control. Sometimes we have to give up the worry and the stress and be committed to pressing forward, even in the face of great adversity. And yes, adversity is sure to come. Nowhere in the Bible does God promise that the Christian walk will be a piece of cake.

But here's the incredible thing. Even though living your spirituality means accepting that God is in control, it doesn't mean that you are never allowed to question or reason with Him. It's okay to wrestle with God. As a matter of fact, He encourages it. Look at Jacob, who wrestled with God after he sent his family across the Jordan River to go meet his brother Esau. Jacob thought he was wrestling with a man, but he was really wrestling with God about who he was as a person. Jacob was struggling with God because he was known as a deceiver and a liar—he was fighting for his identity. And God changed Jacob into Israel.

A lot of Christians are under the impression that they're supposed to be afraid of God. And yes, the Bible commands us to fear God. But the Hebrew word for "fear" actually means that we need to be in awe of Him, of His might. Think of the old paradigm of God as the mighty roaring lion. C. S. Lewis in *The Chronicles of Narnia* described how the children in the book feared the powerful Aslan. He was this big, imposing lion. But at the same time, you were drawn to him; you wanted to reach out and touch him. You loved him. You feared him in the Biblical sense. And this "fear" did not prevent the children in *The Chronicles of Narnia* from asking Aslan: Why are these things happening? And what are we supposed to do now?

In much the same way, God encourages us to call out to Him. There is nothing wrong with saying, "God, I don't understand, why is my son sick?" I called out that prayer to God many times myself. Part of wrestling with God means being very honest, both with God and yourself. Maybe your prayer will be: "God, I don't understand why I am going through this difficult financial time," or, "God, I don't understand why I have to continually fight this addiction. I want to be better, I want to get clean." I know others who have been very sick and have prayed, "Please, God, I don't want to fight this cancer anymore. Please help. I don't understand what You're doing here." Asking these kinds of questions isn't sinful or wrong—in fact, God encourages us to ask them, because they're a part of the intimate relationship He wants to have with us.

Wrestling with God does not mean doubting Him, or doubting that He is Sovereign, that He is Holy, that He is Good. Wrestling with Him means asking, "God, give me understanding, grant me wisdom." And a lot of times, the process of gaining wisdom comes with pain. It's like teaching your kids not to touch the hot burner on the stove because it will hurt them. Sometimes, they just keep trying to touch it until they get hurt. But once they get burned, you can bet they never touch it again.

That's why people need to fail. And that's what frustrates me about our current society: we don't allow people to fail. We all need to fail, because that's how we learn. In my own life, I have learned far more through my failures and through pain than I ever have

> It's only through wrestling with failure that we ultimately discover who we are.

through my successes. It's only through wrestling with failure that we ultimately discover who we are.

Wrestling with Failure

Back in high school wrestling, I made it to the state tournament but lost in the first round because I wasn't mentally prepared. To put it bluntly, I failed. That's how I learned from an athletic standpoint what it takes to be a success. I already felt I needed to put in more time in the weight room; I needed to put more time and work with greater intensity in practices. I couldn't just coast. If I wanted to be the best, I had to be willing to pay the price.

It was the same thing with pilot training. I remember my very first checkride, or competency test, in a Cessna T-37. Checkrides are tests you have to pass to move on to the next phase of instruction. First an instructor pilot from a standardization team gives you an oral evaluation, quizzing you on your knowledge of systems, communications, and emergency procedures—everything associated with that particular aircraft. Once you pass that, you go up and have to show basic proficiency in navigating, communications, and aerial skills to do the different acrobatic maneuvers and different landing procedures. If you can do the maneuvers, you get an Excellent. If you have some glitch or make an error in some procedure, they give you a downgrade.

On my first checkride, I got twelve downgrades. That's a lot. I scored a Satisfactory, which is like receiving a C- instead of an

A. I should have failed. Why? Because even though I'd been in pilot training for a few months and had been doing well up to that point, my heart and my passion were just not there. I had studied and studied and studied, but mentally I was struggling. I was fighting this battle of wanting to play football. I was stationed only an hour and a half from Dallas, where the Cowboys were practicing and playing games at the time. I was dying to be out on the field with them, but I also felt like I had to fulfill my commitment to the Air Force.

I put a lot of stress upon myself with this internal battle—football or fighter pilot. I was fighting the temptation to say, "Screw it. Just go ahead and fail me. I don't even care anymore." I had managed to put myself toward the bottom of my class with that first checkride. So right from the start, I had a big hole to climb out of.

I struggled through that conflict because I had to define, in essence, who I was. Was I Chad Hennings the football player? Was I Chad Hennings the pilot? Who was I? In my apartment, I would cry out to God "Who am I?" It was just like Jacob, wrestling with God, trying to figure out if he was a liar and a cheat, or the father of his people. I was trying to fill this need of what I deemed to be success versus what seemed to be failure. I think that's the point where God allowed me to sit and just struggle to grow on the vine, knowing that I would eventually realize what was true, what was lasting, and what was secure—in essence, where I needed to be.

The answer didn't come until later in life, probably not until I was on the verge of coming back to the Cowboys. So for the next several years, I struggled about who I was as a person. I also struggled with my Faith—not struggled with what I believed, but what my purpose was, my mission here on this Earth. What was I supposed to accomplish? That's where my faith kept me from self-destructing, from blowing up. It was the glue to my fabric, the fiber of my being that kept me from just kicking the ball and saying, "Forget it. I don't want to do this anymore."

My faith is the reason I kept on keepin' on in the Air Force. It didn't make anything better. Frankly, it sucked. It was a bear, mentally and spiritually, going through pilot training. Knowing that God is still there with you doesn't make it any easier. I just kept telling myself that something good could happen from this. I reminded myself that it wasn't going to last forever; that there would be an end to it. It was just like a marathon. You fought all the temptation and the mental urges and you were eventually able to reach the finish line. But along the journey, it hurt. You had to keep taking the steps forward.

Looking back now, I'm glad that I went through that, because it helped me define myself. At the time, I felt like I was failing. I wrestled with that sense of failure day and night. But that's how God tested my faith, and I emerged much stronger as a result.

Living your spirituality means being honest with yourself about how you could do better as you strive to walk with Christ. It means accepting the fact that you will sometimes fail, and preparing yourself to wrestle through that failure. There will always be temptations; that's something we can't control. But if you put on the Armor of God, you'll be better equipped to meet those temptations when they arise. As a result, you'll be far more likely to succeed in every aspect of your life.

Once you've clothed yourself in God's Armor, it signifies that your training has come to an end. You've crafted your character and cast your vision; you've worked on healing your troubled past; and you've developed a work ethic to carry you through tough times. You've committed to a balance of self and dedicated your life to uncovering your purpose, the only true way of finding fulfillment. You are prepared to live your spirituality with valor and courage. Now it's time to get out on the battlefield and put all those lessons to good use.

It's time—for Active Duty.

PART II

Active Duty:
Engaging in Battle

In part I, we talked about the unique challenges of being a Godly man and how to suit up for battle. So you've made it through Basic Training. Well done!

Now I want to talk about how to abide by the Rules of Engagement when you're out on the field, whether that field is your home, your business, your community, or your relationship with God. It's time to prepare your Strategic Plan and lay out the tactics you're going to take to get there.

It's Active Duty. Let's get ready to roll.

CHAPTER SEVEN

Making Your Strategic Plan for Life

To an uninformed outsider, the military looks like it's based entirely on might. It may seem like the most important thing is how big or fast the weapons are. But anyone who's ever studied the military knows that strategy is far more important than anything else.

No battle has ever been won without a strategy. Without an overarching strategy, it's a lost cause. So when it's time for action, strategy is at the top of the priority list.

Your faith walk is no different. In order to carry out the Rules of Engagement on a day-to-day basis, you've got to have a life strategy in place. Everything else—your service to your family, your involvement in your community, your performance at work, and your relationships with other men—falls under your Strategic Plan.

A lot of people get the terms "strategy" and "tactics" confused. These are military words, of course, and sometimes, even people in the military get them mixed up! So before we go further, let's take a moment to define these critically important terms.

Strategy means your overall game plan, your vision, your dream of what you wish to accomplish. Tactics are the means by which you implement that strategy. In a football game, tactics might be an individual player engaging in a particular block, or a quarterback faking a pass downfield and then throwing to the receiver running a crossing pattern. But all of those tactics work together to serve one purpose: fulfilling the overall strategy for the game.

Having a Strategic Plan for your life is essential. As you go along, you've got to be able to look at how any tactical decision you make fits into your Strategic Plan. You don't want to just look back and ask yourself, "Was that necessarily the right way to go?" You need to plan ahead in order to avoid unnecessary consequences. That extra drink you had with the fellas may not have seemed like a poor tactical move at the time—until you got pulled over for a DUI. And you might be able to justify the extra time you spent at work trying to get that promotion—except for the fact that you missed all of your son's Little League baseball games to do it. In the grand scheme of things, was it really worth it?

If we measure these things against our Strategic Plan for our life, our perspective often changes. Our vision gets a whole lot clearer. Suddenly, it becomes painstakingly evident that certain tactical moves just don't fit into our Strategic Plan. And if that's the case—forget about 'em.

Ask yourself a simple question: if this were the end of my life, when I'm looking back from the Endgame perspective on my deathbed, have I led my life the way I'd hoped I would? What doesn't seem to fit is what you've got to fix. That's the beginning of your Strategic Plan. The goal is to continually go back and reevaluate whether or not you're following your plan, and whether or not your tactics are successful. You need to periodically look at yourself, openly and honestly, to determine your strengths and weaknesses. You've got to ask yourself: Is this where I truly want to go? Is this who I want to be?

In one of his many books, management guru Peter Drucker said, "Planning is not masterminding the future. Any attempt to do so is foolish; the future is unpredictable." A Strategic Plan doesn't necessarily mean planning out your life step-by-step. Because of life's uncertainties, that's an impossible task. Instead, your Strategic Plan should outline a kind of road map for how to get to where you want to be. There may be unexpected turns in the road—that happens. But as long as you have your map in hand, you can find your way back to where you're supposed to end up. And when you look back on your life, you can say, "Yes. I made good choices that I'm proud of. I followed the right path."

My goal in this chapter is to help you define your life strategy. Think of your Strategic Plan as the ten-thousand-foot view of your life. By stepping up and looking at the bigger picture, you can be proactive instead of reactive about establishing direction in your life. In this chapter, I challenge you to ask yourself, "What is my plan? And what strategy will I implement to get me where I need to go?"

Defining Your Strategic Plan

Everything I know about having a Strategic Plan I learned by trial and error, mistakes and successes. In the first thirty-five years of my life, I did not have a strategic vision. It was full of interim tactical decisions. Initially, I knew I wanted to do two things: go to college and be a football player. Then, after high school, I set another interim goal for the next four years: to succeed academically and athletically in college. When professional football wasn't an option, I wanted to be the best fighter pilot I could be. Then football became an option again, so I wanted to be the best football player I could be again.

But after all that came to an end, I didn't know what I wanted. I needed to go into business; I needed to make a living, but then what? I bounced between different opportunities and tried my hand at different things, yet a lot of the stuff never really fit who I was as an individual. I learned through pain that those things weren't me. Once I lost money in a business venture, which was a difficult loss. But those things weren't where I was supposed to go. They didn't fit into my Strategic Plan. Of course at that point in my life, I didn't even know I *had* a plan. I was totally lost.

I know I'm not the only man who's felt this way. Why are young men adrift? Why are men in general adrift? Unfortunately, most of us haven't been taught or shown how to plan for our lives. Sure, we may think we have all the answers. We want to tell everybody our opinions. As hotheaded young men, we are typically not, as the old proverb goes, more ready to listen than to speak. And as a result, we miss out on the sage advice that we might get from older men.

In my own life, I shifted aimlessly from one tactic to another, trying to figure out my strategy, for a long time. I was blessed in that the Lord really took care of me. He stood by me, even when I couldn't have named my overall life strategy if my life depended on it. God was patient with me until, finally, after a whole lot of trial and error, my Strategic Plan revealed itself: a heartfelt desire to impact the world (or at least my environment) for God's glory. Our ultimate purpose on Earth is to glorify God—everything else is secondary. It took me a long time to realize my primary purpose. Today, I strive to glorify God in every action—that's my strategy.

I'm not shy about sharing the fact that I'm a Christian and that Christian values define every aspect of my being, from my home to my dealings in the outside world. I want to leave an impact in my sphere of influence, my harvest field, for Christ and for my faith. Ultimately, that breaks down into impacting my family first and foremost, and leaving a legacy to my kids about the importance of balance in one's life. I also want to impact the men in my Wingmen Ministry, the individuals I come across in my businesses, and the greater community with my nonprofit work. These are the tactical goals I employ to ensure that my Strategic Plan is a success. You could call them my milestones. Every man needs milestones if he wants to be able to sit back and assess his life—we all need something to work toward and, eventually, to reach.

My milestones used to be very different from the ones I have today. As a football player, one of my earliest milestones was to achieve success on the football field. Of course after a while, people will forget who you are as a player unless you broke some rush or pass records—and that only lasts until others come along and break your records. When I speak to some of these younger generation kids, they often have no idea who I was as a football player—even though I'm only eight years removed from the game. They were seven or eight years old when I retired, and they don't know me from Adam.

It's the same for such record-breakers as Walter Payton or Jim Brown. Walter Payton broke Jim's record, but many kids today don't even know who Jim Brown was. They might not ever know, unless they're true, avid sports fans. Now they'll know who Emmitt Smith is, but I guarantee in a few years, the next generation is not going to remember Emmitt, either. He'll just be a footnote in the record book.

This is all the more reason why your life should be about the legacy you leave, not the milestones you accomplish. It's got to be about the bigger picture (the strategy) instead of the individual things you do (the tactics). Where do you want to be when you reach the finishing line? Maybe you want to finish the game as a loving husband, a father who raised kids of character and integrity and had a real impact on their lives. Or perhaps you want to be a man who is so well respected in the community that when you shake someone's hand, your word is your bond;

there's no need to have a non-disclosure/noncircumvent agreement in place.

> The question I ask myself is: How do I want to be remembered?

The question I ask myself is: How do I want to be remembered? Do I want to be remembered as a football star? That might be fine and good, but I'd rather be remembered as a great husband, a loving father, and an individual who gave back and impacted my community. These are the things that are set in stone. That's your Endgame.

Building Your Strategic Plan

We've talked about how to define your Strategic Plan and all the reasons you need one. But practically speaking, how do you create an overall strategy for your life? And how do you put it into action?

Your Strategic Plan should be a concise, powerful statement—something you can put on a three-by-five card. It doesn't need to be more than three to four sentences. In fact it probably shouldn't be. The simpler, the better. You can get into the nitty-gritty details with the tactics you choose to implement; your strategy is the larger statement on who you are as an individual and where you want to go with your life.

One individual I know defines his Strategic Plan as: "Being happy and healthy in body, mind, spirit, marriage, and family." That's a great strategy—it's simple but powerful. And when he is faced with a choice that could negatively affect his health or happiness in any of those areas, he knows the right answer.

When you know who you seek to be, it's easy to test any given choice or action against that basic framework. A Strategic Plan gives you the opportunity to consistently monitor your progress and avoid putting yourself in any tactical position that might compromise your strategy.

For example, some men won't let themselves be alone with a female in a room with the door closed, in a business or a social setting. Keeping the door open leaves no opportunity for even the perception of impropriety. This might not always be possible in a business setting, but there are other ways to check and make sure the choices you make at work are living up to your life strategy. You might ask yourself the following questions: Do I really have to take this next business trip? Do I really have to take this next job when the kids are already settled in high school and plugged into their community? You may have measurable results such as getting $20,000 a year more, but is the impact on your family worth that? Moving will really impact their lives. The two have to be measured against each other.

Part of your Strategic Plan must be giving of yourself, because it's not all about us. When you build your plan, think about the other people in your life—your kids, your wife, your wingmen, and your colleagues at work. How will your Strategic Plan touch and affect their lives? Because it's not about money or climbing the corporate ladder; it has nothing to do with material gain or personal accolades or any of those things. Success is a by-product of an entirely different kind of strategy. I didn't play ball with the intention of being an All-American football player. That was a by-product of my going out and wanting to be the best defensive lineman I could be, to help my team win games. Any honors I received or won were by-products of my fulfilling that overarching goal.

When I finally sat down and realized what my Strategic Plan was—in life, not just on the football field—I was able to discern which tactics didn't necessarily complement my overall strategy. That's when I came to the realization that not all good things are necessarily good things for me. If it's something that's going to distract me from my Strategic Plan, I adopt the inverse of Nike's famous slogan—"Just *don't* do it!"

My personal Strategic Plan was forged through trial and error, based on the experiences I had—including both the successes and the failures. That's where I came up with a lot of my philosophy that I'm sharing with you. Looking back, I wish someone had sat down with me when I was a young man in college and said, "You really need to look at who you are. How do you want to be remembered, when all is said and done, and when your mission is complete? What are you going to use to determine that? How are you going to measure whether it was a successful mission, an aborted mission, or a failed mission?"

I never viewed my time at the Academy, my time flying jets, or my time in the NFL as ends in and of themselves. I viewed them as means to an end. Those were stepping stones to a larger platform to impact people on what it means to be a success. How do I impact my family? How do I impact my community and the groups I speak to? What does it mean to be a success?

There's not some magic formula for constructing your Strategic Plan. All you have to do is sit down and take a good, introspective look at yourself. You know the things that are most important to you, the things you truly want out of life. It all goes back to what we talked about in chapter 1: crafting character and casting your vision. What is your passion? How are you going to use your unique God-given abilities to find fulfillment and achieve your purpose?

You may be thinking, "But I'm too old to start working on my Strategic Plan now." Whatever age you are, it's never too late to devise a strategy. It's the old adage: I'm a work in progress. Everybody is. The goal is to realize we will never achieve perfection. The real aim is to get as close to it as we can while trying to learn from the mistakes along the way. So whatever your objective is, make sure you have a Strategic Plan in place. And when circumstances call for it, be ready to change your tactics in order to get where you need to go.

Knowing When to Change Your Tactics

No one can deny the fast pace of our society. Every day we are thoroughly inundated with information from the Internet, radio, television, and print media. Things happen so fast that we get wrapped up in having to make multiple significant decisions in every twenty-four-hour period, or even in a shorter period of time. And where it used to take eighty days to travel around the world, like in Jules Verne's book, we now have the convenience of making that same trip leisurely in only a few days' time—or hours, if your job is flying an Air Force reconnaissance plane.

Society runs so fast that people can sometimes get overwhelmed by all the choices they have to make. And if you don't have a Strategic Plan in place, you'll constantly be playing defense instead of offense. Rather than responding proactively to the fast-paced nature of today's world, you'll be forced to merely react to all the changes coming your way.

But if you *do* have a Strategic Plan for your life, it gives you the ability to immediately assess what is coming up next and whether or not it fits into your strategy. That will tell you whether or not it's something you need to think about. You can probably cut senseless mistakes by 50 or 60 percent, simply by asking: "Does this fit into my Strategic Plan?"

If it doesn't, don't even acknowledge it. Don't go there; don't waste the mental, physical, and spiritual energy even entertaining that bit of data. Only concentrate on those things that fit into your Strategic Plan. If that means being a loving father and husband and spending more time with your kids and your wife, then you can easily make the decision about that extended meeting or business trip being unnecessary. "Nope. Doesn't fit. Boom, I'm gone." Go home and spend the time with your family instead.

Of course as we all know, it isn't always that cut-and-dried. In this day and age, circumstances will often change. Though your Strategic Plan should stay constant, the tactical choices you make along the way may need to be adjusted if you want to achieve your goal. What if your boss is a real slave driver, and if you don't hit all those business trips, you might lose your job? Part of your life strategy is to be a good husband and father and provide for your family. But if you lose your job, how are you going to be able to uphold that part of your plan?

If your tactics aren't working for the greater benefit of your Strategic Plan, it might be time to change them. Maybe now is the time for you to look for a different position or a different job, or to have a heart-to-heart with your boss. Explain to him the situation—tell him you're only willing to work so many hours because you need the flextime to spend with your kids. You're offering a solution, a compromise. If he says no? Now you're at a crossroads. But because you have a Strategic Plan in place, you can measure this job against your overarching strategy. Is this job worth spending x amount of time away from your family each week?

Or maybe you work for an unscrupulous boss who goes to strip clubs, requires you to wine-and-dine individuals, or keeps requesting "just two more hours" of work. If these offers are going to put you into harm's way, then you have to ask yourself if it's really worth it. Is this job working against the strategy you've set for your life? If the answer is yes, then maybe this job no longer fits into your Strategic Plan.

There is nothing wrong with changing jobs or even careers. Change only becomes a problem when it endangers your sense of self and what you are aiming to achieve with your life. The bottom line will always be: as long as something does not compromise your Strategic Plan, your tactics can change based upon the economy, environmental influences, or anything else that life throws your way.

In the Air Force, there's a saying: "The key to air power is flexibility." You want to win the engagement, or you want to get your munitions on target. When I was in England flying, the weather often caused low visibility, particularly in the fall and winter months of the year. The purpose of the A-10 Thunderbolt II was to provide close air support. That meant we had to practice continually dropping bombs or shooting the GAU/8 Gatling gun. Our mission was to drop bombs on the range.

At the range, we would brief specific targets beforehand, but once you got to the target area, the weather was not always suitable for flying. You'd go down to your weather minimums—your limits. If you pushed it below the minimums you would be putting yourself in harm's way. You would need to go to an alternate range, and if that range wasn't suitable, you'd go to another one, and another one, until eventually you'd get to one where you could go on and employ your tactics to complete your mission. Or go home to fly another day.

The same thing happened a few times when I was flying in northern Iraq. We had to get to our target area, but due to low visibility and low weather ceilings, we weren't able to dip down; the mountainous terrain wouldn't allow us to safely get down to find a way into the pockets of Kurds to help them or escort the relief supplies in. So the mission would be scrapped and we would come back another day.

We also occasionally had to forgo our missions because of political problems. If a particular area of Iraq was "hot," we couldn't go there. We were briefed to go in, but if there was some scuffling going on they didn't want the presence of aircraft overhead.

In every one of these instances, we had to change our tactics. Sometimes, changing your tactics is the only way to survive. But no matter how much we had to adapt our tactics, our strategy—to do our duty and serve our country—never wavered. So just remember: be flexible. As long as your Strategic Plan stays constant, you'll remain on the path to ultimate success.

Fulfilling God's Strategic Plan

I've definitely witnessed some pretty incredible things over the course of my life. But for me, these are just some of the "tools" God has given me so that I can live out my Strategic Plan: speaking and motivating other people by talking about my experiences. They're no big deal—it's no different from what a teacher does, or a policeman, or the guy who works the nine-to-five job in the office down the street. But for some reason, pro sports and the military—the two fields in which I've had most of my experiences—are perceived by a lot of people as being "cool."

It's my belief that we tend to put too much emphasis on athletes. I, personally, am totally in awe of concert pianists. That's something I wish I could do: play a piano. I'm also in awe of the academic or the writer, who can so eloquently take thoughts and ideas and put them down on paper. That's talent and I respect it—it is so cool.

Thank goodness not everybody enjoys football. As a football player myself, I'm entitled to say that! I thank God that people enjoy music and the arts. We are all diverse. It takes all kinds of people to fulfill God's Strategic Plan, and no one group is more special than another. As a result, everyone's plan is going to be different. And it's precisely the breadth and diversity of our own life strategies that allow us to fulfill our destinies as believers and followers of Christ.

We're not all created the same and we're not all given the same vision. That's why we have to come together with other believers. No effective strategy ever worked in a vacuum—not on the football field, in battle, or in our walk with Christ. God says that together with our fellow believers, we form the body of Christ. I may be the arm, someone else may be the knee or the foot, but we all have to work in concert to make our community, our world, and our faith walk successful and operational. It doesn't matter if you've got a killer Strategic Plan—if you try to do it all on your own, it just isn't going to work.

Not everybody can be the star quarterback, but at the same time the star quarterback can't do it by himself. You need everybody from the trainers to the equipment guys to the guys on the practice squad who don't even get a chance to dress in the game. You need the guys on special teams and backup players, you need the starters and the coaches. Everybody has a role to fill. In the successful teams, individuals operate within their own role. They know who they are, they know their purpose, and they know their goal and their vision. They know their tactics, and they also know that their tactics are going to change along the way.

We need to teach our kids that you don't have to be famous

or in the limelight to be cool. My son's in a wheelchair, so he doesn't have to be a football player to be successful. He doesn't have to try to fill my shoes just because it was what I did. You have to find the abilities you have, and be the best you can be with them, no matter what they are.

Having had the experience of having a son who was very athletic as a young boy and then watching his physical body slowly deteriorate made me adjust my priorities—or what I *perceived* were my priorities. It's important that you pull the reins back on the expectations you heap on your kids. Is it really important that your kid plays select soccer or baseball? Should you pay some $2,500 to $3,000 when they don't find their calling in sports? If they want to play and they're good enough, then by all means, proceed. But if you're the one spending three or four nights a week pushing your child to go to practice and he doesn't want to go, aren't you damaging your relationship with that child? Whose dreams are you really pursuing, his or yours?

Part of fulfilling God's Strategic Plan is recognizing that though we are diverse, each of us is worthy, and every single one of us has an important part to play in glorifying the Lord. What that part entails depends on you.

Your Strategic Plan is what defines you, what gives your life shape and meaning. The tactics you choose provide the color, depth, and texture of your existence. In the following chapters, we'll look at the tactical components of your strategy: the individual ways in which you can emulate Christ in your dealings with your family, your wingmen, your money, and others in your community.

You need both a strategy and tactics to live the life God intends for you. But at all times, remember to keep your eyes, heart, and mind on your Strategic Plan. That way, at the Endgame ceremonies of your life, you will be able to look back on what you have created and say, as God Himself said in Genesis 1:31, "[He] saw all that he had made, and it was very good."

> You need both a strategy and tactics to live the life God intends for you.

CHAPTER EIGHT

Serving the Family

If you're like most of the men I know, your family plays a significant part in your Strategic Plan. These are the people who are most precious to you, the ones you love and treasure in your heart of hearts. They are also the people who have been given to you by God so that you may set a Christlike example for them to follow. Your service to your family should be your very first priority.

To begin our discussion on a man's responsibilities to his family, we have to pick up our Bibles and turn all the way back to the first chapter of Genesis. That's where God introduces us to the original family, the very first married couple: Adam and Eve.

The Old Testament makes it clear that God is both masculine and feminine in nature. So when God formed Adam and Eve, He made them in His likeness. Genesis 1:27 says, "So God created man in his own image...male and female he created them" (NIV).

From the rib of Adam, God created Eve to be a helper, with

equal rights. Adam was a Godly example of leadership, while Eve served him with humility and meekness. Together they were a unified body, a perfect state without animosity. There was balance between man and woman, and man did not lord over woman as if he were a king and she his servant. Before the fall in the Garden of Eden, both Adam and Eve had equal access to the Lord.

We all know what happened next. God told Adam, "You may eat from any tree in the garden, but not from the tree of knowledge of good and evil, lest you die" (see Gen. 2:16-17). So Adam went home to Eve and relayed the message—with one small change. When he told his wife about the tree, he said, "You cannot eat of it nor touch it, lest you die." From this, we can surmise that man, even before the fall, did not have great communication skills.

When Eve took the apple, he stood idly by. And when she offered him a bite, he accepted. At no point did Adam step into the leadership role that the husband is meant to have.

How does this apply to being a husband and father in today's world? Here is the parallel: just like God is the head of Christ and Christ is the head of the church, a man is the spiritual head of his household. He needs to set the leadership example, not only by bringing in an income and being there for his children, but also by setting a spiritual example for his family. Christ served mankind by giving His life for the church. Similarly, a man needs to be willing to give his life in exchange for his family.

In this chapter, we're going to talk about how to emulate Christ in your relationship with the people who are nearest and dearest to your heart: your wife and kids. And in a fallen world where the family is under constant attack, your role as husband and father has never been more important.

Your Role as a Husband

After man was forced to leave Eden, men and women became divided by nature. We can all attest to the difference between the sexes—probably more than we would like! Men are into the nuts and bolts of making things work, while women are more intuitive—they're more into feelings and following their instincts.

Today we are in a culture war. Men and women's roles are constantly being questioned. In the context of marriage, we're relentlessly redefining who and what we are. Who am I supposed to be? What role should I be fulfilling? We face so many consequences because we, as Christians, have not stood up for what we believe. There's as much divorce within the church as outside it.

Sexual promiscuity is at an all-time high and it is changing and harming relationships. Men are not viewing their wives in a realistic manner. Instead, they have some virtual image of perfection in their eyes that can never be satisfied. You can't escape your mind. That draw, that physical yearning, is always there. It makes you want more. You're likely to fall into a deep spiral because you're not getting any fulfillment from it. That's why pornography is like a vacuum that continues to pull you down.

God created man and woman the way He did for a reason: one male and one female coming together in a holy union. That's why man should leave his mother and father, cling to his wife, and the two shall become one flesh. But our culture has become more and more narcissistic. We are less interested in forming a partnership than we are in doing what we want. Society's focus has turned inward, each person thinking, "Me! Me! Me! Satisfy *my* needs first."

If you look at the hierarchy of needs between a male and female, a woman's top needs are communication and security, while a man's top needs are physical satisfaction and a need to be honored. Those with the current worldview want their needs met first. This creates a chasm between men and women, with both genders focusing on fulfilling their own needs first. He watches pornography to satisfy himself, ignoring her need for communication, and she cannot be intimate with him, unable to honor a man who is in essence having an affair, if only a virtual or mental one.

In the Old Testament, God gave Moses Ten Commandments to live by, including "Thou shalt not commit adultery." Later, Christ said, if you even look at a woman with lust, you're creating an adulterous relationship. Christianity really raises the bar. But the great thing for us as Christians is that Christ already paid the price for our sins. We simply have to accept that our penalty has been paid. That doesn't mean you're given free range to have lustful thoughts whenever you please. While we live in God's grace, we are still obligated to work with and through Christ to gain release from that sinful bondage. We still have to be willing to fight our own base desires so that we can be Godly husbands to our wives.

In order to get beyond the chasm between being two separate entities—a husband and wife—each has to be willing to give themselves to the other person first. This is not about you. It's about the other person. As leaders, we must be servants first. And as husbands, we are in special need of this mentality—the mentality of a servant-leader.

I've had several men come to tell me about their experiences when they took on the role of a servant-leader in their marriage. Each one told me how they made concerted efforts to truly nurture their wives. They found the time to sit down and actually talk, either in the morning, after work, or simply before the kids started running around. Whenever they could find a quiet moment to spend together, they focused on nurturing their relationship. They realized how important it was to let their wives know they cared about them. While before, they provided for their wives' material needs as the only priority, those men now understand that what gives their wives true security is genuine nurture—communication and consideration. A man's wife reciprocates this security by providing the honor and physical intimacy *he* needs.

In a healthy marriage, it is important for both man and wife to value and respect each other's opinions and input. When I introduce my wife to a potential business partner, or show her a prospective business opportunity, I ask her to feel it out. She may say, "You know, this doesn't set right with me." If asked why, she might tell me she really doesn't know. She can't put her finger on it. Something inside her, her intuition, tells her it isn't a good deal, or the person is untrustworthy.

I might say, "The balance sheet looks perfect. I did a background check on this guy and he's fine." In the past, I have trusted my cognitive ability and, thinking she doesn't know what she's talking about, moved forward. It has almost always ended up coming back to bite me. The deal goes south, or the guy ends up proving himself dishonest. I have subsequently learned to listen to her. If one of us doesn't have a good feeling about something, if we're not in unison going forward, we don't do it. We delay the decision.

My wife and I were married in 1990. Together we have seen couples' self-serving relationships and marriages crumble and dissolve. The common denominator is whether or not they truly care for each other, and whether their views are selfish or giving. We need to give of ourselves to each other. Not just the physical aspect, but the mental and the spiritual as well. When these things are out of whack, it causes strife in the house. When Dad or Mom goes on a rampage, each family member walks around on eggshells. When things work, however, it makes a huge difference. The house is filled with happiness. The family is more jovial, and it's common to hear laughter ring through the halls.

Your Role as a Father

In recent years, the familial roles of father and mother have become confused, changed, and twisted. I'm sad to say that as Christians, we have not stood our ground. We have become distracted by society's push away from what God intended—the gender roles He planted in our very natures. It's no wonder so many families are falling apart today. We've wandered very far from what God intended the family to be.

Women are nurturers by nature. Even when they are children, girls tend to fulfill these roles by playing house and cradling their dolls for hours on end. They have an innate need to provide comfort, to be the housewife, the mother, the caregiver. Conversely, little boys play with guns, wrestle, and fight. These roles are instinctive and natural. But when we start to redefine these roles, we become confused about who we are. Wives are suddenly putting in just as many hours at the office as their husbands, and the family is suffering as a result. It's not just the current generation of men and women who are totally confused about the roles of men and women—it's the next generation, too.

Why shouldn't kids grow up thinking that the most important role a woman can play is to care and nurture for her children and her family? That's what God intended. Let us keep in mind the value of a woman who is a caregiver. If she received payment for all her areas of expertise—chauffeur, maid, cook, doctor, counselor—she'd be paid well north of six figures. So why does society send the message to our little girls that they are second-class citizens if they choose to stay home and care for their families? The role of caregiver is, in fact, the most important role. If the cultural family unit disappears, what do we become? We need to stand up for what is right, for what is good, for what is noble. The role of the woman as wife and mother is paramount to the strength of the family.

Though a woman's role as mother is incredibly important to a family's growth and well-being, that's only half of the equation. A marriage is a balance between the male and the female, and you make up the other half. Your role as a father is to lead your family. Sadly, men have abdicated their roles as spiritual leaders in today's world. Many people argue that the Christian church today is too effeminate because men have checked out of the church. Who teaches the Sunday school classes? Women. Who does the majority of the charity work? Women. Men have become increasingly irrelevant in the spiritual development of their children. And that's why our society is becoming more and more out of balance.

It's too much to ask women to play both roles of mother and father when it comes to offering children a spiritual path. Your job is to complement everything your wife gives and contributes by being a Godly husband and father. God privileges a father's love for his children—in fact the first time the word "love" appears in the Bible, it refers to the love of a father for his son (Gen. 22:2). As a father, your duty is to love your children fully, wisely, and respectfully. It is your responsibility to set the spiritual tone for the rest of your family.

My wife and I split parenting right down the middle. It's a zero sum game; we each have equal influence with our children when it comes to the decisions we make. As parents, we're pretty calm. We may know how to push each other's buttons, but it takes much more to get us upset with our kids. We're trying to literally live a Christlike example. It's not a switch you just turn on, and it doesn't happen overnight. You must keep a watchful eye out on which way you are evolving as a father. Are you going up, or are you going down?

I do not view my role as a husband and father as a benevolent dictatorship. I am not a king, my wife is not my vassal, and my kids are not serfs. We treat it as a democracy. My wife and I both have input, but the decisions are made mutually. It is, however, the husband's role to set the strategic vision for the family. I'm willing to give my life for my children and my wife out of love and respect. This love and respect, as well as the example Christ set for me, help guide me in setting the right spiritual tone.

One of my favorite stories in the Bible is in John 4:46–54. These verses tell a story about a nobleman with a sick son. The nobleman pleaded for Christ to come heal his child before he died. Jesus simply said, "Go your way; your son lives." When the man returned home, he discovered that his son did indeed live. Verse 53 continues, "So the father realized that *it was* at the same hour in which Jesus said to him, 'Your son lives.' And he himself believed, and his whole household" (NKJV). This is the perfect Biblical example of a man leading his family—of how a father's faith in Christ ultimately led to the salvation of his entire household.

As the leader of the household, your faith walk sets an example for the rest of your family. You must show your wife and children what it means to be a Godly man. They say that when a child is first to take Jesus into his heart, to believe fully and completely, there is a slight chance that the rest of the family will follow. If the wife comes to faith first, the chances of her family following increase. But when the husband comes to faith first, the chance of familial faith is at its greatest level, as his family is likely to follow him as their leader. This is just the way God set things up in His world.

As the leader of your family, you must continue to set the spiritual tone in all aspects of your life and explain to your children why God wants us to follow His path. Sometimes having those discussions will be difficult. I once sat down and explained to my son the physiological changes a person experiences when they view pornography. A male, when sexually aroused, emits hormones, primarily testosterone, which fuel aggression and sex drive.

God created these hormones and sex drive for a man to desire and have pleasure with his wife, creating a physical bond. And God created that chemical bond so that when you are sexually aroused with your wife, you also create a spiritual bond. During premarital sexual relations, or while looking at pornography, you create a chemical bond with that person or image imprinted in your brain. It's as strong, if not stronger, than any chemical dependency because it's constantly with you. If memories of those past experiences come back, and a man continues to view pornography, he's doing irreparable harm to his marriage.

Though my son is a long way from thinking about marriage himself, he listened carefully to everything I said during that conversation. After we were finished, he had a new understanding of how and why pornography is so damaging to the life God intends for us to live. I was able to set the spiritual tone on a topic that plagues many men—a topic that all too few men broach with their sons.

The Five Tenets

When I first met my wife, we were paving different religious paths. She was raised Catholic and I was raised conservative

Lutheran. We decided to raise our children in a non-denominational Christian format. This was the first real compromise we made. It took a long time for us to work through the religious baggage, and to filter through the differences between the denominations in which we were raised to find what we both knew to be scripturally true—to find the path we would take as a family. This journey put stress on our relationship, but we continued to search the Bible for answers regarding our roles as parents. The process evolved over many years, but the Bible has always stayed at the forefront of our quest to set a Godly example for our children.

In the world today, the Bible is a best-selling book. That doesn't necessarily mean people are implementing all of its lessons—although the world would be a much better place if they did! But in our family, the Bible is definitely the most important book and the only one by which we strive to model our lives.

There are five tenets from the Bible that I impressed upon my children. We have now made it a fun exercise that whenever I ask, "Now kids what are the five truths," they take turns rattling them off individually. I'd like to share them here with you.

The first is, "Fear of the Lord is the beginning of wisdom." We all start with God. We must respect God and honor Him for who He is. Like we discussed, fearing God doesn't mean being literally afraid of Him. It means being in awe of all He is and all He does.

The second tenet is, "He who walks with wise men will be wise." As I tell my kids: choose whom you associate with very carefully because they can either lead you to folly, or lead you to wisdom. If my children hang out with the wrong crowd, there are going to be consequences—and not just from their dad! But if they choose wise people as their friends and cohorts, they, too, will be wise. It is equally important to choose wise role models.

The third tenet is, "Do your best in all things." My kids must give their best effort in everything they attempt. That doesn't mean I expect perfection from them. None of us is perfect. But I do expect them to give their all in all the activities and projects they undertake—not for their own glory, but for God's.

The fourth tenet is, "Life is a series of choices—choose wisely." We make choices every day. What I tell my kids is: you have to learn to make good ones. Do you sleep in? Do you get up? Do you choose to watch TV? Do you read a book? Do you finish your homework? Or do you call your friends? As you get older, the decisions you make have more consequences involved.

The fifth and final tenet is, "God disciplines those whom He loves." This can be a hard one for kids to grasp, because nobody likes to be disciplined. But it's important for my kids to remember that Mommy and Daddy follow this example. We discipline them because we love them. I don't view discipline necessarily as punishment, but as guidance. I remind my kids that I have been on this Earth longer, and have more experience and wisdom by default. I'm simply providing counsel. I discipline to help them make the right choices for themselves.

These five tenets form the crux of my parenting technique. You may not choose the same ones, but I strongly encourage you to go to the Bible for guidance. Just be watchful that the rules don't overpower the messages you're trying to impart. The rules can easily become idols. You begin worshipping the rules and system rather than worshipping God. Christ confronted the Pharisees about this. "You're tithing even the mint in your garden, but you aren't taking care of your own parents. You can teach and prophesy, but without love, you're nothing." Yes, you need rules in place for your kids. But those rules should always come from a place of fatherly love. Think of them as the tools for expressing your Godlike love for your children.

When you show your children what is right, they will see it. When they grow up and embark on marriages of their own, they will have already experienced the necessary training in doing what's right. And someday, when they have children, they will be able to model Christlike behavior because of the model you set. Instilling values in your children when they are young is the only way to stop the dangerous addictions and spirals before they start, and to keep them from passing down from generation to generation.

It is your responsibility to model Christ's love to your family. If you honor and love your wife and love and lead your children, they will know what it means to be a man of God, what it means to be a Christian husband, a Christian father, a servant-leader. Remember to always embody that balance of leadership and service, because truly serving your family means giving freely of yourself.

> It is your responsibility to model Christ's love to your family.

CHAPTER NINE

Enlisting Your Wingmen

Going on Active Duty can't happen without your fellow brothers-in-arms. So when it comes to living a life for Christ, one of the most fundamental tactics we have to adopt is learning how to build healthy, supportive relationships with other men.

As men, we need someone to be there constantly: someone we can confide in, someone we can have that "Jonathan-David Covenant" relationship with, someone with whom we can share our hopes, our dreams, our aspirations, our failures, our temptations, and our sins.

I call it the Wingmen Ministry.

We first talked about the concept of wingmen in chapter 2 in terms of healing your troubled past. But that's not the only reason your wingmen are invaluable. We are made for relationships. Men need other men. Men can stand shoulder to shoulder, back to back, in the open. We need strong masculine relationships, friendships, bonds. Think about the different levels of athletic competition: junior high, high school, college, and professional. Relationships are forged in these situations between men. Under stress, the players lift weights together, sweat together, bleed together. While working together toward a specific goal—victory on the field—the players share life's experiences together.

To keep certain aspects of our lives in shape, to keep us out of that potentially endless downward spiral, to help us get back to healing, we need relationships. Those relationships come in several forms: a relationship with God, a relationship with a spouse, and relationships with other men. But it is your relationships with other men that mold and forge the bonds that will help you through life. The male relationships I have today with my former football teammates, as well as from the Air Force, are some of my closest.

When you're flying, whether you're doing training missions or are in combat, the success of your mission is interdependent upon your wingman. You're coordinating, taking care of one another, and watching each other's backs. Your ability to come back from the mission—and the success of your mission—is dependent upon one another. When one watches the other's back, you both get there safely. Whether it's a two-ship or four-ship formation, you aren't thinking about fighting for your flag or for your country; you aren't thinking about your family at home. During your mission, you are dedicated to your wingman. You're flying for him.

In everyday life, we're working toward the same basic goals. We each have our unique visions, our purpose, our Strategic Plan. But we need men around us with whom we can lock arms as we battle the world—especially in our battle as Christian men against a sinful society. This battle is weekly, daily, hourly. In order to be successful, you must work with like-minded teammates to ensure a victory. Imagine a fighter squadron. You're working toward a common goal, the success of the mission. You work as a group, you live as a group, and you walk away with relationships that follow you through life.

The same is true in football. To win the football game, you're constantly making tactical decisions, knowing that the wrong one may lose you the game and let your teammates down. It's the same thing with life. We all want to be successful fathers, successful husbands, and successful sons. We don't want to let our teammates down.

We're all going to have moments when we're tempted by sin or frustrated by the choices available to us. Maybe you're faced with a dilemma that you *know* goes against your Strategic Plan, but you feel helpless to make the right decision. This is where you need other men. Men who can say, "Hold on, cowboy, don't go there." Those relationships you forged in the trenches are the ones you need to call on when the going gets rough.

The world tells us that to be a man, you must show no weakness. It says, "A man betrays nothing but success and strength." We are made to believe that "real men" are never vulnerable. A vulnerable man is a "girly man," a loser. He's portrayed as whiny and wimpy.

Lucky for us, these common perceptions are way off base. In reality, true warriors are the ones who talk and share, who open up. No man, not even Rambo, has ever won a war alone. In past times, warriors sat around the campfire after the day's battle and talked about the experiences they had and the things they saw with their fellow warriors.

This is what you and your wingmen should do. You must be willing to let down your facade. A real man makes sure that he has a few close confidants to whom he will show his vulnerabilities as well as his strengths. Forging those bonds is what makes for a strong and unbreakable team.

In this chapter, I'm going to share with you the truth about male bonding—and why your wingmen are an indispensable part of your life.

Defining Friendship

Even in our forefathers' generations, it was hard to define friendship. There are different levels of friendship, after all. For example, you may have bowling buddies or fishing buddies. These are usually superficial friendships. You go, you hang out, but you would never open up to these men. While these relationships are fine—most men have them—these are not the relationships that will strengthen who you are as a man of Christ.

Look to your other relationships for a wingman—say, to your best buddy, the man you grew up with, the one you hung out with every day during the summer. You knew everything about each other and were the best of friends. This is your wingman. This is the person you want to open up to, the person you want to keep close. The bonds you forged as a child, playing together, working together, still hold true today. These are the bonds you want to work to make even stronger.

The world has sped up and while we're trying to keep up with it, it becomes easy to get lost in the rat race and confused by the noise. As my wife has said at times, "It feels like we are hamsters on the hamster wheel"—and no one can get off. The faster you go, the faster you'll have to continue just to stay up. If you stop, you're going to get hurt. So we keep up with the rat race in order to succeed, in order to meet social expectations and be the provider that we're supposed to be. Society dictates all the things we have to do, and it sets a pretty high standard. To meet that standard, something's gotta give.

Unfortunately, what typically gives first is the ability to meet with friends. We stop sharing because it takes too much time. Time, though, is a commodity. Just like money, it's an asset, and a valuable one at that. So it's important that you manage your time like you would with any other investment. We each need a small group of friends who know each other well. Make sure you invest the time in keeping your inner circle close.

Look at your calendar. You can immediately tell what you feel is important and what you feel isn't. If you spend fourteen hours a day working, ten minutes with your kids, and then maybe five minutes a day talking with friends, it's clear you're not focusing on your relationships. Again, we're back to priorities. You have to take a stand. What is important to you?

It's obvious that we need friendships in life. Life is a marathon, not a sprint. Even when running the race alone, you need support—a coach, a trainer, and a person to bring you water during the run. You know you'll have water at that six-mile point because of that support. We need support or the world will keep chipping away at us. We're fighting a battle, and we have to keep our hands up to withstand the fiery darts the enemy serves us.

A boxer in a boxing ring who drops his hands gets knocked out. When we get to a point where we are punch-drunk from fighting too many worldly foes, we need our friends to help us with defense. And your wingmen will be the first to come to your aid.

Acceptance, Affirmation, and Accountability

In the introduction of this book, I mentioned something I call the real AAA—Acceptance, Affirmation, and Accountability. When you enlist wingmen in your life, keep these tenets at the forefront of your relationship.

The wingman's role as an affirmer is especially important. In a hierarchy of what a man needs from his wife, to be affirmed and honored ranks just as high as his need for sexual intimacy. That's why it's so important for a wife to honor her husband. But it is just as important for a man to be affirmed by his friends. And the affirmation we receive from other Christians fills a need that a woman can never fill.

In order for your wingmen to affirm and accept you, as well as to hold you accountable, you have to be willing to be honest about both your past and your present. Perhaps you have done something you're ashamed of, or perhaps you were victimized when you were a child and you are still carrying the guilt, shame, and resentment. Maybe you didn't have the relationship you wanted with your father, or you never connected with your brother and these issues are still affecting your sense of being. Too many times men are not affirmed that these things are okay.

But here's the good news: your past doesn't matter. Our mission as wingmen is not to dwell on the past but to press toward the goal of motivating our fellows to be the men that God is calling us to be. You must remember that your Heavenly Father forgives you, if you ask for it; as do I. I won't bear any grudges against you. I affirm you. I'm going to accept you for who you are in God's eyes. I won't judge your past. Let's work on the go-forward.

If you had an addiction in the past that you're still dealing with, you're not living the life Christ would want you to. Yeah, I'm still going to accept you—but then I'm also going to hold you accountable for your actions. In that way, I'm going to help you become the man you have the potential to be. It's not exclusive; it's a mutual, symbiotic, synergistic relationship. I can be a confidant, a mentor, or whatever role I need to play. No matter what, we're in this fight together. The past is past and don't worry about it. Let's not ask, "Why?" Instead, let's ask, "What next? Where can I go from here?"

Masculine relationships are our way to embody a fierce brotherly love for other men. In Biblical times, the leaders of each clan would come together and forge a covenant. Basically, they would say, "I will protect you; you will protect me." They would forge this covenant with an exchange of blood and sacrifice. They were forever sealed together. That's what Jonathan and David did.

Jonathan was Saul's son, born to be the next king as far as the world was concerned, but he realized God had called upon David to be the next king. There was no animosity, there was no jealousy—they were truly happy for one another. They cared for one another, looked out for one another, and loved one another in the platonic sense. Jonathan and David's affection for each other was truly a brotherly love.

The universal concept of male bonding is a Biblical truth, but the world took it and bastardized it to fit its own meaning, turning it into a joke or for use in advertising. I occasionally get some razzing about the whole wingman concept because of that Budweiser commercial: a guy goes into a bar with his wingman and asks his buddy to help him out by hanging out with the ugly girl so he can be with the more attractive girl.

That's not what a wingman truly is. That's why I use the analogy of going to war. When you're in battle and it's a life-or-death situation, you want guys around you who would be willing to give their life to save yours. What greater love is there than an individual who gives his life for a friend?

Wingmen Can Save Your Life

When you're in an emergency situation, your wingmen will come up and check you over. They'll do a combat or battle-damage check, which means the wingman basically gets behind and looks under and behind your aircraft. He checks you over to make sure there's no battle damage. Every time you come out of a combat area, you need to do a battle-damage check.

When I had my engine failure in the A-10 that I spoke about earlier, my wingman made sure I wasn't leaking oil or experiencing any other malfunctions. He made sure I was stabilized.

Finally we were able to go in to the divert base. To do that, you set yourself up on a straight-in approach that is just a long, gradual descent to the runway. And the whole time I was setting up there, my wingman was following in a fingertip formation, right there beside me the whole way down.

Things happen so fast in the cockpit while you're flying. They train you to always maintain aircraft control when you're in an emergency situation and deal with things as need be. So your wingman is there to support and help you, flying beside you and slightly behind, watching you. He's there to help you communicate with others on the outside, with air-traffic control, and to make sure that everything is taken care of. As you touch down, he maintains in the air, does a go-around, and lands behind you.

We do the same thing in the secular and noncombat world. When you're dealing with something difficult, you need to keep a friend next to you. He accepts you, affirms you, and holds you accountable. He makes sure you're ready, asks how things are going, and asks if you are spiritually fit. He coordinates and assists you when you need something. He's there—not necessarily to fix things, but just to be there to support you. And then he helps you get on the right path as you continue to deal with your situation. He helps get your feet planted back on the ground.

We must remember to keep our wingman close. Keep him flying right beside you the whole way, and keep yourself flying beside him, doing what needs to be done by coordinating with him. These bonds help you, prepare you, and make sure you're flying straight. They help in every aspect of life, but especially in your communications with others: your wife, your kids, your family, your other friends, your business. These all-important relationships get us through life.

Wingmen Can Help You Fight Temptation

When it comes to temptation, your wingmen are absolutely vital. Everyone's hotspots are unique—we all have specific things that lure us down the path of sin. These temptations need to be recognized so they can be proactively withstood, and so that you can call on your wingmen to help you avoid the positions of weakness where your hotspots or temptations are.

If you're struggling, thinking you won't make it through the week, you need that wingman you can call on at anytime to share and talk it out with. Pick up the phone and say, "Hey, I'm struggling with this problem this week. For whatever reason, I'm getting attacked in this area of my life. Could you pray for me, man? And let's meet tomorrow, because I just need to talk this out."

Perhaps you have an issue with pornography or an extramarital affair, or you know alcohol is your weakness. Search those memories from when you were in college, or from when you were a young person, before you were married, and remember all the things you did that brought on those temptations. Heed those memories, but don't dwell on them. It's important you don't let yourself be put in harm's way.

Even when there's just a slight change in your circumstances, it's surprisingly easy to do what you normally wouldn't do. If you're away on a business trip, for example, it's all too easy to allow yourself to be tempted to have more than one drink with dinner, or to chat up a pretty woman at a bar, or to visit those Internet sites. In those situations, your wingman should be first on your speed dial. Call him up, explain what's tempting you, and trust in him to help you steer clear of it. In fact this is one instance where it's perfectly acceptable (and even advisable) to turn your back and run.

Remember the example of Joseph from the Bible, who actually runs away from temptation. Joseph, brought to Egypt as a slave, had risen to the role of Pharaoh's top economic advisor. Potiphar was one of Pharaoh's lieutenants, and Potiphar's wife sought to seduce the young, handsome Joseph. Joseph had to run away from her as she was literally ripping off his clothes. Temptation was as powerful for Joseph as it is for many of us men today—but he made the choice to run away.

Every guy goes through the same things. You can share with each other little things that help. For example, I had a friend who had a problem dealing with lust—and who hasn't, at some point in his life? He would be walking down the street and see a beautiful woman. It's okay to admire her for her beauty, but problems start when you take those second and third glances and you start undressing her with your eyes. When you start admiring her more than just for her beauty, that's where it becomes an issue of lust.

When this friend would start to feel himself taking more than that first glance, he'd place his finger beside the bridge of his nose and turn away: a gentle reminder to not go there. He told me, "It's a physical reminder of how to deal with lust."

Of course, one morning when he had just started to work out on the treadmill, this beautiful, drop-dead-gorgeous woman started working out next to him. Twenty different treadmills in the area, and she just happened to take the one right next to him. He's thinking, "God, I can't look over at her," so he does the thing where he puts his finger on his nose and turns his head. Sure enough, there's a mirror right there and he's looking right at her; he can't escape it.

Sometimes what we laugh about today are the situations where we needed a wingman there to help, especially in a situation where we'd done everything we could to alleviate that temptation. We may have little tricks up our sleeves to help us, but we still need men around to pull us back and keep us in check—to assure, affirm, and accept us while holding us accountable.

———·———

God doesn't tempt, but He does allow us to be tempted. First Corinthians 10:13 says: "No temptation has seized you except what is common to man. And God is faithful; he will not let you be tempted beyond what you can bear. But when you are tempted, he will also provide a way out so that you can stand up under it." In other words, God will always provide a way for us to escape. And one of those ways is our wingman.

Satan is much stronger than we are on our own. Don't make the mistake of just sitting there and saying, "I'm a guy! I can take it. I can walk into that bar, or walk into that business meeting with that unscrupulous individual, or open up that e-mail I know I shouldn't. I'm strong enough; I can do it and not fall to temptation." No matter what we think, we just can't do it. No man is strong enough.

We *can* walk away from temptation, but we need other men to help us learn how. One of the things that keeps a sin a sin is the sense of fear and shame we feel. We are afraid to let other people in or to expose our sin. We're ashamed to open up because we're afraid of the reaction, afraid the facade we have built will crumble and our reputation will be tarnished beyond repair. We have a sense of shame for what we have done in our past indiscretions.

But all of that changes when you have wingmen in your life. We need that wingman, that trusted male individual to expose our shortcoming to the light. It needs to be uncovered so that we have the opportunity to realize that the fear and shame we feel about our sin do not have a hold on us.

The two greatest commandments are "Love the Lord your God with all your heart and with all your soul and with all your mind and with all your strength," and, "Love your neighbor as yourself" (Mark 12:30–31). It is a combination of your relationship with God and your relationship with other humans—specifically other men—that helps you recognize your hotspots and strengthens your faith. When you withdraw, when you go back to that John Wayne syndrome and don't have other people, other men, in your life, then you're susceptible to sin. You become a one-man Rambo fighting a battle, and the chances of your having a successful mission are very slim. You may be able to hold off the enemy for a

> We *can* walk away from temptation, but we need other men to help us learn how.

short period of time, but after a while, you can't withstand the onslaught.

Building Wingmen Relationships

There is a vacuum in each of us, a deep yearning to be accepted, whether or not we're ready to come to terms with that. We want and need to have close personal relationships. Unfortunately, the world doesn't always accept that men have this need. We have all been teased at some point by siblings or had a bad experience at school—maybe you didn't have parents who could model this for you—but even if you don't realize it, you still yearn for that connection. There's an innate need to have those relationships and to have that acceptance, to affirm and get beyond that facade.

I've seen it many times, over and over again. Men who had come to the point in their lives where they realized they were missing something. They had a whole lot of friends and fishing buddies, but they didn't have the in-depth companionship they desired. They felt they had to keep up a facade, and were afraid of people finding any weaknesses or chinks in their armor. What they needed was to be able to get real with somebody, to be transparent.

How you achieve those connections, first and foremost, is through prayer. Pray about it. Whether you're a new believer or a mature individual, God will provide. In my wingman group, we had a gentleman who had just moved to the area and was part of the military. He said, "I've been praying for a group of men for several months that I could have as wingmen." God orchestrated that he meet an individual who talked about our Wingmen Ministry. He came in and found this was exactly what he was looking for.

A good starting point is to attend your church's men's associations. And, like the man who found his way to my wingman group, commit it to God through prayer by saying, "God, I want a friend! I want a confidant, a warrior buddy. I want someone who will battle with me, who will have my back and stand shoulder-to-shoulder with me. Someone who's not afraid of listening to me and telling me the truth." If you make finding other Christian men a priority in your life, God will honor that commitment.

It's not like I went out and found some guy and unloaded on him. I forged those relationships over time. It's a matter of (1) a willingness to be vulnerable, (2) finding someone who shares your likes and dislikes and with whom you have common ground, and then (3) over time, little by little, building up that bond.

A lot of men's groups, like the Wingmen Ministry, started off with a group of guys who said, "We're gonna commit to one another. What's said here stays here and nothing is off limits. We're going to meet regularly, we're going to pray for one another, and we're going to have fun as a part of each other's lives." Then, over time, months down the line, those bonds began to really formulate. It's almost like they hit that tipping point where someone is vulnerable and says, "Okay, I'm willing to take a risk. You've shown me that I can trust you."

Then, bang, it's like a dam bursting and all the weight you've been bearing on your shoulders is gone. You're now sharing that burden with one another. Share your burdens with Christ; His yoke is easy. And then share them with each other, as it says in James 5:16: "Therefore confess your sins to each other and pray for each other so that you may be healed. The prayer of a righteous man is powerful and effective."

———·———

Over the years, I've had friends from the Air Force Academy, the Cowboys, my business, and other places. And every time I've moved, I've changed my group of friends. But when I go back into those friend circles, if the bonds were truly close and authentic, it's like I never left. At my twenty-year college reunion, I ran into some old classmates and we ended up meeting for lunch. I hadn't seen some of those guys in years, but we just picked up right where we left off. There's a sense of security, knowing that, hey, I can still trust them. They know intimate things about me and vice versa. We still have that bond.

Today's multimedia culture can be a real pain, but it also has some benefits. We're a mobile society: many people change jobs or move houses every few years. But thanks to the interconnectivity of the modern world, you can now stay in touch with the important men in your life. Even when you move, you can still maintain your friendships through text messages, e-mail, or conference calls. It's all real time now; teleconferencing is a cost-effective way of keeping in touch where you can see each other. It's almost like actually being there. Even e-mail is almost considered obsolete. Kids today text or interact on MySpace or Facebook to maintain contact.

If your wingman moves away, you can still stay in touch using all the different means we have at our fingertips today. If you're flying through town and know someone from your past may be there, you can get together for dinner or just to check in. Just because you've moved doesn't mean you can't still maintain those relationships.

But you do still need somebody with whom you can physically hang out—a wingman who you can actually sit across the table from and get real with. All the teleconferencing in the world can't take the place of real face-to-face connection. We need to be able to look into somebody's eyes and see for ourselves how they are doing. E-mail is so impersonal. Talking over the phone is a little more personal, but it's still not the same as looking into somebody's eyes to see where they're at, and to see whether or not your wingman is being truthful about everything being okay.

Your relationships with your wingmen should be one of the top priorities in your life. No one can follow God alone. Make time for your fellow brothers in Christ, and you'll always have backup when you need it most. Your wingmen are your fellow warriors, your confidants, your best friends. The more you spend time developing those relationships, the richer your faith walk will become.

CHAPTER TEN

Men and Money

Every business seminar and MBA program drills the importance of measuring results. Somehow, men have carried that notion over into their personal lives, where the only area they measure on a regular basis is their bank account. This has led to the belief that our value as individuals is tied to our net worth.

Men seem to view money as a measure of success, the basis of the popular bumper sticker, "He who dies with the most toys wins." Too many of us get caught up in the belief that the important things in life are not just money, but the other "riches" that seem to come packaged with it: fame, prestige, entrance to elite social circles. Nothing could be further from the truth.

In this chapter, I want to talk about the attitude we as Christian men should have toward money. I also want to emphasize wealth over riches. I define "riches" as materialistic notions, while "wealth" is your legacy—your character and the set of values that you pass down to your kids. Theologian D. L. Moody said it best: "If I take care of my character, my reputation will take care of me."

Character Lasts...

How you spend money is a good indication of how you spend your time, and time is just as much of an asset as money. We need to step back and look at what metrics we're using to measure our success. Think back on your Strategic Plan. Is it just to accumulate wealth? God wants us to be successful, but not solely in matters of riches that serve no purpose in His kingdom. Our life here on Earth is a proving ground. We're here to use our talents—all the ones we've mentioned throughout this book—not for purely material gain, but for the common good and to fulfill God's purpose in our lives.

Biblical times weren't so different from today. The character and nature of man remain the same, as do the major societal issues we face—sexual purity, marital relationships, and, yes, money. Consider the parable of the widow's offering, in which a poor woman is commended by Jesus for having given, proportionately, more than her wealthy counterparts. Christ made an example of her, saying she gave all that she could give and then some. That's how we are judged. Not by the amount of our giving, but by the amount in our hearts.

Jesus knew that, as stewards, men would struggle with the concept of money. We are equipped to oversee and subdue the Earth, but also to be good stewards of it. In performing our stewardship, we transact business, which invariably involves money. And it's our attitude toward money that drives our true success. Sex and money are the two main aspects in today's society that we are hammered with more and more, because they are both innate in man's nature. And when it comes to money, you will be judged as to whether you view it as a tool or as the Endgame.

If your identity is serving the almighty dollar, you will never reach satisfaction or fulfillment. I've met many individuals who are never satisfied with their riches. They seek only to accumulate more and more, despite what studies have shown: that beyond the most basic point of having enough money to survive, greater riches have no correlation with greater happiness. Of course we didn't need scientific studies to know that—it's always been a universal truth that money can't buy happiness. Happiness is found in the giving, not in the receiving.

"I ain't never seen a hearse with a luggage rack," sang George Strait—and with good reason. When you die, you won't be taking it with you. Most likely, your descendants will get whatever the government doesn't, but for you, your riches are fleeting. Your character and good name, however, will live on well after you've gone. Therein lies the true wealth to be passed down to your kids, and for generations thereafter.

The value of character was well known even back in the time of Ancient Greece. That's what the heroes of the day strived for: to be known eons later. The Greek epics talked about a person's name as character. The Ancient Greeks wanted nothing more than to be remembered well after death, because they understood that material things alone would not create a lasting memory. Rather, they endeavored to be remembered for serving their communities or city-states, fighting gloriously in battle as Achilles did in the *Iliad*, and fulfilling their roles as husbands, fathers, and friends.

We are familiar with this concept today since it's mentioned many times in the Bible. In 1 Timothy 6:17–18, Paul speaks to Timothy in his Epistle:

> Command those who are rich in this present world not
> to be arrogant nor to put their hope in wealth, which
> is so uncertain, but to put their hope in God, who
> richly provides us with everything for our enjoyment.
> Command them to do good, to be rich in good deeds,
> and to be generous and willing to share.

. . . Riches Don't

Money causes emotional stress for people, myself and my peers included. We have more riches than the average guy, but it could all disappear just as easily. Just one bad quarter in the stock market, and we could be the guy hawking hot dogs in the bleachers.

Time and again I've watched professional athletes go from riches to rags, just as a hastily gained inheritance is soon squandered. If you don't earn it and you don't garner the discipline along the journey of accumulating it, you can't respect it. This is why so many trust-fund kids who inherit the riches but not the wealth (the legacy and character) from their parents so often fritter it away.

I learned a great lesson from my father—that as a farmer, you're not going to get rich, but you can make a great living. You'll make a 5–7 percent return every year, and that's what you go for. Slow growth. That's the best way to build a life, and not just life savings. Inheritances, lottery winnings, and the high salaries of sports stars will not last. Yes, people win the lottery and their lives are changed overnight, but they end up being broke within the next eighteen to twenty-four months, because they didn't earn it and gain the discipline along the journey to accumulating it. If there's no foundation for accepting wealth, it won't last. In much the same way, if there's no spiritual foundation for building a life, then, once again, we're just building on sand.

The parable of the Prodigal Son tells the story of a son who squanders his early, unearned inheritance because he didn't appreciate what those riches represented. When he returns home humbled, his father welcomes him with open arms and restores his position in the family. The parable reinforces that wealth—not riches—is the legacy with the true value to be passed on to our children.

Giving Freely

We Americans toil endlessly to take control of our own destiny and to achieve riches. Most of us want a nice house to raise our families in, a safe car, and freedom from constant stress about our finances. And that's fine. After all, that's part of the American dream. But we also need to understand how giving can not only make others happy, but also bring happiness back to us many times over.

"Remember this: Whoever sows sparingly will also reap sparingly, and whoever sows generously will also reap generously.

Each man should give what he has decided in his heart to give, not reluctantly or under compulsion, for God loves a cheerful giver" (2 Cor. 9:6–7). That last part says it all. We should all be cheerful in giving. We've got to realize that when God blesses us, He wants us to utilize the riches we have earned.

On Judgment Day, when you're sitting before Him and are asked, "How did you utilize the opportunities and materials with which I've blessed you?" you don't want to reply that you've been hoarding them to yourself and your family. God wants you to share these riches with others through philanthropy. He wants you to continue to strive for success in your business and to also help others through business—think of it as being a capitalist with a heart. It's using the blessings you're given to create blessings for others.

I do believe in profit. I do believe that we deserve the earnings we get from doing our best. But we must also ask ourselves, at what cost am I amassing this fortune that I'm not sharing with others? What is this costing my heart? There's a right way and a wrong way of winning the game of life.

The Old Testament spoke often of tithing, which is the practice of giving 10 percent of your earnings to the church. And while the Lord doesn't need our money, He does love a cheerful giver. I try to avoid being legalistic or pharisaical in defining the tithe in terms of a percentage. The percentage isn't important, rather the act of freely giving. I try to give more than 10 percent, and I have friends who give far beyond that—I know some people who even reverse the ratio and give away 90 percent while they only keep 10 percent! And God continues to bless them.

My point is not to get wrapped up in the numbers. I once asked John Weber, a former chaplain for the Dallas Cowboys, how much we should give. "Save all you can, give all you can, and spend all you can," he replied. I thought that was a wonderful answer—as long as you keep the three areas balanced. I personally believe that you don't even have to tithe the whole tithe directly to the church and not give to other organizations out of the tithe, though I have some pastor friends who certainly disagree with me on that point.

Bottom line: is your heart in the right place when you give to those in need? Are you giving to widows and orphans as the Bible directs us, or are you giving only for the tax deduction? What if your donation doesn't qualify you for a tax deduction— say you've bought shoes directly for a needy child or given bus money to a man who's lost his wallet? Because that type of giving freely is an even better check of what's in your heart.

Malachi 3:10 reads: "'Bring the whole tithe into the storehouse, that there may be food in my house. Test me in this,' says the LORD Almighty, 'and see if I will not throw open the floodgates of heaven and pour out so much blessing that you will not have room enough for it.'" This is the only place in the Bible where God says to test Him. He's basically saying, "I dare you to see if you can out-give me." There is some debate as to whether the storehouse is considered the church. The point is, however, that God wants us to give of all of ourselves—our time, talent, and treasure.

> The point is, however, that God wants us to give of all of ourselves—our time, talent, and treasure.

God is gracious, but you can't let that be your sole reason for giving. You can't give just to get back. After all, God isn't operating a hedge fund with a guaranteed return on your generosity. At the same time, He also doesn't want you to not give simply because you feel that your riches are yours and yours alone. We have to split it down the middle. We should give because we want to and because that is God's calling to us. It helps to view our riches in the light that what we have is only because of His blessing. It was never ours to begin with—it belonged first to God. We are simply stewards of the riches and the material blessings that God has lent us, and how we utilize those material blessings is how we will be judged as men.

Of course these guidelines are not strictly for men. They're life principles for everyone to live. A woman's attitudes toward money should be no different from a man's. And before the two marry, they should make sure they're compatible in this matter, or there's going to be a lot of arguments when it comes time to balance the checkbook, even in the case of tithing.

Husbands and wives typically split household responsibilities, and they can do this with finances, too. Unlike other responsibilities, finances require a lot of communication in order for the household to operate smoothly. Otherwise, one spouse is left handling the bills and, when something happens—loss of a job, injury, or even death—the other one feels lost not knowing how they got into that financial state. As in all things, there needs to be communication.

You want the best for your family. You owe it to them to be responsible in all areas of your life, including financially. This means you shouldn't spend what you haven't got. Don't buy that bigger home or forgo life insurance if it puts your family's future at risk. If something were to happen to you, where would that leave your wife and kids? You have to think beyond the immediate gratification of making a dollar. That's part of your legacy to pass on. And in light of the economic crisis we're facing, there's no better time to whip your financial habits into shape.

In 1 Corinthians 3:11–15, God says:

> For other foundation can no man lay than that is laid, which is Jesus Christ. Now if any man build upon this foundation gold, silver, precious stones, wood, hay, stubble; Every man's work shall be made manifest: for the day shall declare it, because it shall be revealed by fire; and the fire shall try every man's work of what sort it is. If any man's abide which he hath built thereupon, he shall receive a reward. If any man's work shall be burned, he shall suffer loss: but he himself shall be saved; yet so as by fire. (KJV)

Here's my paraphrase of this passage. When it comes time to be judged, you will be tested by fire. What perishes in the fire will be your worldly things, while what survives the fire will be your character, your legacy. But if all you've done is accumulate riches, they will be destroyed. You will be saved, but your reward will not reflect the blessings that God has poured for you.

God has heaped blessing upon blessing upon us. Yes, sometimes those blessings come with a dollar sign. But the greatest gifts God bestows upon us are not green; they can't be put in a bank account or a hedge fund. I count my greatest blessings as my relationships with my wife and family, my bonds with my wingmen, and the daily opportunities God gives me to fulfill my Strategic Plan by sharing my life story with others. By putting these aspects of my life way above making money on my priority list, I'm storing up the kind of riches that really matter.

As Jesus tells us in Matthew 6:20-21, "Store your treasures in heaven, where moths and rust cannot destroy, and thieves do not break in and steal. Wherever your treasure is, there the desires of your heart will also be" (NLT).

Focus on the true and lasting desires of your heart, and you will accumulate a true and lasting wealth worth more than all the money in the world.

CHAPTER ELEVEN

Serving the Community

When I talk to groups, I talk a lot about the concept of service. Every individual wants to lead a life of significance—they want their life to count. We all want to be part of something that's greater than ourselves. We want to look back on our lives and see that we have made a difference. Some people choose to fill their inner need with things that are for selfish gain: money, fame, or social status. But others choose to answer the call of service. It's a Biblical principle that the greatest person needs to be a servant first.

I've played on championship teams, made more money than I ever thought I would, and rubbed elbows with some famous and phenomenal athletes and celebrities. But, truly, those aren't the things I look back on and see as being the most significant moments in my life. It was my time as a young lieutenant in a fighter squad, flying both combat and humanitarian missions, when I learned the importance of teamwork through service. It was about the camaraderie and the reliance upon your wingman in a training or combat mission. It was the sense of purpose. It was there that I learned about what is truly important and what makes a difference.

When I first walked into the Cowboys' locker room and I transitioned to the NFL from the Air Force, I was intrigued that the men there were more interested in my experiences flying than anything else. Sitting around the locker room or weight room, they wanted to hear my stories of what it was like to be in a combat zone. They wanted to know what it was like to "put it on the line." They wanted to know how it felt to serve.

The desire to put it on the line and test your metal is innate in every man, whether it's on the athletic field, in the classroom, playing in a symphony, or on the battlefield. Women don't understand that desire, but it's a rite of passage for men dating back for millennia. We all want to know if we have the right stuff. Some people faced with the opportunity to serve answer the call, whether in military service, charity service, or service of some other kind. Others choose to watch from the sidelines and never get in the game.

Now's your opportunity to get in the game. In this chapter, we're going to talk about the ways in which you can be a servant to the other people in your life. Service to community is the last Rule of Engagement, the final component of your Game Day as a Godly man and follower of Christ. Your community doesn't have to be physical—it could be a service organization, a charity you believe in, or a certain group of people like single moms, disadvantaged kids, or war veterans. The important thing is that you find a community to serve and get plugged in. And if you've never heeded God's call to service before, don't worry: it's never too late to start.

Why We Must Serve

The concept of service can be summed up in John 3:16: "For God so loved the world that He gave His only begotten Son, that whoever believes in Him shall not perish but have eternal life" (NASB). That is the concept: God gave. What greater example is there of service than God giving His only son, and Christ giving His own life?

Even from the beginning of the Old Testament, way back in Genesis 1, God showed us His devotion to service: He gave us life. Later on in the Bible, there are multiple examples in both the Old Testament and New Testament regarding the care of widows, orphans, and those less fortunate. Matthew 23:11, in which Jesus addresses the pride of the scribes and the Pharisees, says, "But he who is greatest among you shall be your servant" (NKJV). This was in direct response to the Pharisees' attitude and sense of elitism, and we see time and again in the Bible that Jesus speaks out against pride and praises those who serve.

But serving doesn't mean being subservient. As we saw in chapter 8, a father assumes a servant-leadership role, meaning that you serve while you lead and lead while you serve. For example, one of the ways I model Godly service to my kids is to enlist them in my philanthropic passions. I've found that one of the most effective ministries in my own life is not only being a servant-leader to my family, but actually engaging them in charitable endeavors by my side. If you can involve your family in your service work, you'll be doing double duty: serving, and providing a role model for your kids at the same time.

When your kids see you giving to others, they learn that it's not always about them. They also learn that service is not like a job where you are materially compensated for your efforts. You're modeling that servant attitude, showing that you're doing it because you care and because it's the right thing to do. I tell my kids, "I'm doing it because I'm modeling God and Christ's behavior, which they exemplified for us and which we are called to do."

One of the greatest gifts I can give to my family is the opportunity to serve. One of the charities with which I work has a holiday program, where those in need can stop by for a turkey or a food basket from the pantry. My kids and I have worked side by side for three hours in an afternoon handing out these baskets to people in need, or serving in a kitchen for those who can't afford Thanksgiving or Christmas dinner. Even though the kids give up their time, they have an incredible amount of fun, especially when they see how grateful people are for something that they themselves would normally take for granted. I was proud to see my children jump wholeheartedly into the endeavor, and I knew the sense of accomplishment they felt for having served others. I can tell you that my spirit soars when I give to others, whether I'm giving of my time, my talent, or my treasure.

As a society, we are extraordinarily philanthropic with our treasure, time, and talent. But it's not enough to write checks. I see life as a constant growth process involving learning and giving back. And the more you can give back to your community, the more God will bless you.

How We Should Serve

We've established why we should serve. But how do we do it? How do we make a positive impact on the lives of others?

The best tip I can give you is: start small. The way you really make a difference, the way you really change the world, is one person at a time. We no longer live in an era when young people go to the city gates to sit at the feet of wise men. Today, it is the wise man who must seek out his mentees. We can't wait for these opportunities to come to us—we have to seek them out, in order to maximize the gifts that we have been so freely given. We have to be proactive in seeking out opportunities to serve. For example, there are people in Alcoholics Anonymous who don't sit idly by in meetings hoping that a newcomer will come over to them and talk. Instead, they'll approach the newcomer, offer their phone number, and even ask the newcomer for his number—and then reach out to keep the connection alive.

I'm involved in a charity called Christian Community Action (CCA), which I believe has found a truly effective way to help those less fortunate. Unlike a lot of other charities, which are set up only to fulfill an immediate need, Christian Community Action's goal is to stabilize an individual's life by helping him or her to find a job and a home. When an individual's needs are met, he or she can begin the journey of meeting different milestones and eventually reach the point of complete

> The way you really make a difference, the way you really change the world, is one person at a time.

independence. Program participants learn the discipline necessary to maintain their standard of living.

If they choose not to work for that next milestone, however, they are no longer eligible for the program. In other words: if you don't work, you don't eat. Some other charities simply give food or clothes with no accountability on the part of the recipient, which only enables the behavior that put them in a position of need to begin with. Christian Community Action follows the old adage: give a man a fish, and you have fed him for today; teach a man to fish, and you have fed him for a lifetime. CCA's primary demographic is single moms, who enter the program with the goal of reaching independence. By doing so, CCA is also giving the gift of self-respect.

Honor and self-respect are particularly important for a man. When you take away a man's ability to care and be a steward, to fulfill his role in subduing the Earth and providing for his family, you're killing his soul. But by giving a fellow human a hand up, you're giving much more than any material good you could donate.

The end product of service must always be the recipient— never ourselves. Yes, we will reap tremendous rewards through our service, but unless we are helping the less fortunate to escape their downward spiral and improve their behavior, our service is for naught. We must strive to ensure that our service makes a difference in their lives so that they can improve.

Serving is crucial to our spiritual well-being, but unless we do it correctly, we may actually cause more harm than good. For the sake of the person we're serving, we don't want to further enable any destructive behavior. And for our own sake, we want to make sure that we focus on what is important to us so as not to spread ourselves too thin.

I learned the hard way to focus on only those charities about which I'm most passionate. When I took on too many, I not only disrupted my personal balance, but I wasn't doing much good for any one charity because I had too much on my plate. You could feasibly be involved with a different philanthropy every night of the week, but then you would be neglecting your own needs and the needs of your family.

When I played for the Cowboys, I received two or three requests a week to speak to a group or donate to a charity—all of which I found incredibly worthy. But as my commitments piled up, I soon found that the charities that meant the most to me weren't getting the attention they deserved, and my own needs were falling by the wayside. I soon learned to say, "I believe in your mission, but I am involved in these other charities, and that is where I dedicate my time. Thank you, but I simply can't accept."

Is it better to volunteer your time and energy, or to write a check? Is it better to have that one-on-one relationship, or to provide financially? The answer is that the world needs both. You just have to find the right outlet that suits both your personality and your passion. If you're an introverted businessman, then a one-on-one relationship probably isn't the best choice of service for you. But if you're an outgoing individual who delights in getting your hands dirty or meeting new people, then you'd probably do well at a Habitat for Humanity event or becoming a Big Brother. Feel where God is leading you, then search your heart and spirit to decide how you'd best like to serve.

I want to encourage men to find their individual passion to serve. Different men find it in different forms of service. If you grew up in a single-parent family, you may find that you wish to help single moms. In that case, donating time or money to an organization like Christian Community Action might be perfect for you. If you enjoy working with kids, you might want to concentrate on child-focused charities. Perhaps you love the outdoors, in which case you might want to serve your community by improving the environment and cleaning up our parks. If you enjoy working with your hands, try building homes for Habitat for Humanity. Sports lovers can chaperone a Big Brothers/Big Sisters group to athletic events, or get involved with community weekend events to teach kids athletic skills. There's a multitude of ways to serve.

My former head football coach at the Air Force Academy, Fisher DeBerry, grew up in a single-parent home. His mom worked long hours, so he was raised primarily by his grandmother. This experience later stoked his passion to start a foundation for single moms, in which the organization helped their kids through athletic programs, scholarships, and various other family-geared practices.

What is your passion? Where do you want to serve? Where do you want to give back? When you've discovered the right outlet, you won't care if serving means getting up at 6 AM on a Saturday. You'll be so excited about the opportunity to give that you won't mind missing out on your one day to sleep in.

———·—

I sit on the board of directors for a nonprofit called Happy Hill Farm that aims to help at-risk kids. This is my passion—working to help the most innocent and vulnerable in our society. For the kids that Happy Hill Farm helps, there are usually very few choices available. There's rarely anything better than the child welfare system, which I find leads furthest down the spiral—from probation to prison—with little hope of ever escaping the system.

Happy Hill Farm's goal is to remove the child from the at-risk environment, whether that be one in which they're being abused, getting into trouble with the law, exposed to drugs, or something else. Once at Happy Hill, the kids are bound to the Farm's rules, but they are rewarded for good behavior by receiving additional freedoms. The Farm doesn't condone risky or bad behavior, but they do practice positive reinforcement.

The organization is a fully accredited K–12 school, with a wide array of extracurricular activities, from sports to agricultural programs such as 4-H and Future Farmers of America. But at its core, Happy Hill Farm is spiritual, a nondenominational Christian organization with mandatory chapel and a foundation built on morals. A few years ago, Dr. Phil highlighted Happy Hill Farm on his show, calling it the best facility of its kind in America.

Unfortunately, so many deserving institutions are facing financial or legal difficulties and having to shut their doors, putting an even greater strain on the field. The need far outweighs the supply of facilities like this, and that's where I try to make a difference. If this is an area that even remotely interests you, please consider volunteering. We need your help!

If you need further encouragement, think of this story. A few years back, as a favor to a friend of mine, a few of my Cowboys teammates and I went to a family amusement center as part of a function for abused and neglected teens. After a few moments interacting with the kids as a group, I noticed a young girl about thirteen years old, and something told me that I should make an effort to approach her. Within moments, we were laughing and playing video games together. I didn't think much of it at the time, probably because I was having as much fun as she was.

The next day my friend sent me an e-mail telling me how this girl had been severely sexually abused by her father and had not interacted or spoken with anyone since she had joined his group. But after our visit, she had opened up and started to rediscover some of herself. I couldn't believe that my little interaction with her had led to such a profound change. I hadn't gone with the intention of impacting someone's life. I just went because it was the right thing to do and because my friend had asked me. But for her, it was a breakthrough. You never know how you can impact the life of a child.

The Upshot of Service

Although we should not look at service as something that will give back to us, I can tell you that it does—often in unsuspecting ways. In my service work with soldiers returning from Iraq and with at-risk kids here in Dallas, I feel that whatever I give is a small fraction of what I get back.

By serving, you're providing a role model for children—yours and anyone else's who might learn of your endeavors. Your work just may be the inspiration that spurs others to take action and serve. And your example of service is part of the legacy that we pass down to our kids, the wealth that you store up by setting a Godly example for your family. That legacy is what's going to outlive us—those are the treasures you store up in heaven. Performing service is equivalent to paying into your retirement account in heaven. That's where you'll reap dividends twentyfold.

The attitude you have when performing service is important. There's a right way and a wrong way. Bringing attention to yourself should not be part of the game plan, because it moves the focus from those who need it to you. If you want to comport yourself humbly, follow the words of my high school coach, Reese Morgan: "Act like you've been here before." In other words, brush off any praise as if the feat you've just accomplished is no big deal.

You can carry that advice into all aspects of your life to keep yourself from getting a big head. That's exactly what I did when I scored my first and only NFL touchdown. As I ran into the end zone, I couldn't believe what I'd just accomplished. But instead of getting cocky and beating my chest, I kept my cool, with the help of Coach Morgan's words ringing in my head: "Act like you've been here before." That touchdown was my service to my team, my coach, and the fans out in the stadium. So instead of a preening peacock display, I simply handed the ball to the referee and started to jog off, allowing for a brief hand gesture to signify that the Cowboys as a whole were number one.

Of course a few seconds later, I realized that in the NFL, the player who scores the touchdown can keep the ball! So I ran back to the ref to retrieve my memento. I still have that ball, and when I look at it, I'm just as proud of how I carried myself as I am of the feat that earned me my prized keepsake.

———

I can't tell you how many times I've used my football connections in my volunteer work. In 2007, I helped organize an event in which a foundation paid for a suite at a Cowboys game for a group of disabled veterans from the Brooke Army Medical Center. Southwest Airlines flew up more than a dozen vets and their significant others for a fully comped day. These guys laughed and joked, hooted and hollered, because they had a moment to forget about the pain. I felt wonderful at having had the opportunity to be part of that happiness, to have helped these men—if only for a day.

For some men, the call to serve is so strong that they do so as their full-time job, whether that is in the military, public service, the ministry, or any number of other professions. Sometimes that commitment comes with risk to one's own personal health, but the call is so great that it cannot be denied. That is why I consider these men and women heroes. They serve knowing that their only compensation may be grave physical injury, but they do so anyway because they know how much their service will benefit others.

Some of the most heart-wrenching experiences I've had were visiting the wounded soldiers and Marines at Brooke Army Medical Center, the Center for the Intrepid in San Antonio, and Bethesda Naval Hospital. On one visit, I sat in a hospital room with a young man who had lost much of his skull in an IED explosion that blew his Humvee to God's creation. He was alone with his mother, having just been left by his wife who couldn't stomach being married to a grotesque monster. Many of the other patients had amputations or severe burns, injuries that they'd have to live with the rest of their lives.

The despair in the building was palpable. You could almost hear the soldiers' thoughts: What is my family going to think? How am I going to support myself? How could I have gone from being a vibrant, healthy man to having such a horrible physical impairment?

And yet, despite all their doubts and fears, they still want to give back. They continue to want to serve. For some of them, service is just a natural part of life.

Once they've recovered, many disabled vets go on to start their own businesses. But no matter what other pursuits they undertake, the majority of them also stay engaged to help counsel and support their other brothers who are going through the same trauma they experienced. I find it incredibly motivational to see someone who's been knocked down continue to want to serve.

That's where I count my blessings every day. These men and

women have inspired me to continue serving the people in my life. We have to think of all the families whose fathers, sons, daughters, and wives have come home broken—or haven't come home at all. That's where we must all be wingmen, to reach out to those young men and women and help them and their families down the rocky path to recovery.

This same degree of service and giving could be with any emergency preparedness organization, such as firefighters or police. I often think about the 2,998 people who went to work on 9/11 and never came home. Many of those emergency preparedness workers didn't return because they gave. I've often asked myself that if I were in that situation, would I be able to give the ultimate? If I were to see someone in need of help, would I give my life in exchange for theirs? I hope that the answer is yes, because that is the ultimate sign of service. I'm humbled to even think about Medal of Honor winners, those recognized by our country for having given their lives freely for someone they perhaps didn't even know. To me, they are the true heroes.

As the final component of Active Duty, serving our community is our Endgame as strong Christian men. It's the ultimate way to go out there and give it your all—to really go out with a bang. But as I constantly remind myself, service is not about self. No matter how proud I am of my accomplishments, I am determined not to let pride get the best of me. Public recognition is not the goal. All of my football accomplishments mean nothing compared to the times that I've given selflessly, expecting nothing in return.

Service is about acting with character and integrity and setting a Godly example. It's about giving back to others in a way that enriches and transforms their lives. And most of all, it's about doing what's right—not because we'll be rewarded, but simply because it's the right thing to do.

> Service is about acting with character and integrity and setting a Godly example. It's about giving back to others in a way that enriches and transforms their lives.

Redefining Manhood

What does it mean to be a man? Is it as simple as a recipe calling for one-third John Wayne, one-third John Gray, and one-third John the Baptist? In a complicated world, I don't think it's quite that simple. But when it all comes down to it, who are we, really? How do we define ourselves as Christian men?

They tell the story of a Dallas Cowboys' fan visiting San Francisco who was walking in the park when he saw a large dog break free from his chain and attack a small child. The Cowboys' fan rushed over, subdued the dog, and held on to it until the parent could take the frightened child away and until animal control could remove the dog from the park.

A reporter happened on the scene and said, "What a great story! I can see the headline now—49ers' Fan Saves Small Child!"

"But I'm not a 49ers' fan," the hero of the story admitted.

"Okay," the reporter said quickly. "No problem. I can see the headline now—Raiders' Fan Saves Child From Vicious Dog Attack."

The man shook his head sadly. "I'm not a Raiders' fan either."
And then he told the reporter what team he really rooted for.

The next day, the headline in the newspaper read, "Redneck Kills Family Pet."

It's a funny joke, but there's a real lesson behind it—that sometimes our whole identity gets wrapped up in the team we root for. That's why it's so important that we align ourselves to God's team. That's how we should define ourselves as Godly men. The only place we can find our true identity is in the Lord who made us, and in Christ whose example we strive daily to follow. That's what makes us strong, compassionate men who live a warrior's life of faith and courage. And, as I've learned along the way in my life, strength doesn't mean dominance; masculinity without compassion is unbridled ego, and faith without works is dead.

In this book, I haven't been proposing a "new paradigm" for manhood. Instead, I've sought to illustrate the fact that the classical definition of what it means to be a man really is the right definition. We were never meant to go it alone, to steer a course away from our fellows, our families, or from God. Instead, the true definition of manhood encompasses a variety of traits—strength tempered by thoughtfulness, the desire to accomplish tempered by the need to be a part of a community, and above all, finding common ground with other men walking a path to faith.

Unfortunately, the way I define manhood actually *has* become something of a redefinition, because somewhere along the way, we lost track of what it truly means to be a man. It isn't easy to be a "real man" in society today, because the pressure to adhere to a feminized version of manhood is so strong. At the same time, our advertising culture encourages a Peter Pan–like stance toward adulthood, creating a generation of males who do not feel any particular need to grow up, take on responsibilities, and walk their faith.

For men today, the choices are complex and the temptations to live down to one's basest nature, instead of up to one's highest and noblest purpose, are often overwhelming. I empathize with the men in Wingmen Ministry who have made choices they regret, because certainly I have made similar choices, too. There is no shame in falling down. The only shame is in falling down and not getting back up.

Charles Barkley memorably told us in a Nike ad more than a dozen years ago that athletes are not role models. If anything, I believe my experience on the fields of athletic competition, from the wrestling mat in Iowa to the Super Bowl, give my ideas an audience. But if I don't walk the talk, if I don't live the virtues I espouse in this book, then I really am no role model. I hold myself out as an example of an imperfect individual seeking to emulate the example of the only perfect role model: Jesus Christ.

> It is Christ's generosity, His loving kindness, His presence, and His willingness to connect with me at all times—especially at dark and dangerous times—that give me an example of how I am supposed to live as a man.

It is Christ's generosity, His loving kindness, His presence, and His willingness to connect with me at all times—especially at dark and dangerous times—that give me an example of how I am supposed to live as a man. Am I there for myself, living up to my standards? Am I there for my family, providing emotional, spiritual, and financial support to those I love? Am I there for my friends, serving as a wingman to other men, and allowing them to play that role in my life? Am I all about me, or am I all about the greater good?

The hand that is most open to give, not coincidentally, is also most open to receive. I'm not advocating a life of monastic self-lessness. I believe God wants us to be in the world, on the court, in the arena, meeting our responsibilities. If we're looking for someone who is hurting, we don't have to look far, it's sad to say. There are so many opportunities for us to step outside ourselves and find common ground and compassion for those around us, whether it's the veteran returning from Iraq or Afghanistan with PTSD, the friendless young man in the inner city, or a brother in Christ who has temporarily lost his way.

The remarkable thing about human beings is that we are wired to feel good when we help one another. It's actually been documented that the body's internal chemistry set produces the same upbeat feelings when we help someone—the so-called helper's high—that mimics almost precisely the runner's or athlete's high. Bet you didn't think you'd read a book and find Chad Hennings advocating people get high! The serious point is that God divided man into men that we might help each other. And in helping each other, we find our true purpose, our true calling, our true path, and our true faith. Most of all, we find ourselves.

It's time for the Peter Pan generation to come to recognize that there is enormous satisfaction and strength in growing up, in serving others, in leading our households, and in turning our hearts to Jesus Christ. That's been my experience, and that's what I've sought to convey in these pages. These are the Rules of Engagement for living life as a strong and Godly man.

I hope you find the same satisfaction and strength on your path to living in Christ's example as I have on mine. Our Heavenly Father is waiting patiently—for His sons to become men.

I salute you on your journey.

Chad Hennings, founder of Wingmen Ministries, is best known for his role with America's Team, where he spent his entire nine-year professional football career, retiring in 2001 with three Super Bowl rings.

An accomplished lineman in high school, Hennings was offered full scholarships from universities across the nation. Instead, he chose to attend the U.S. Air Force Academy, where he racked up numerous honors academically and on the gridiron. Among these was being named most valuable athlete at the Academy, as well as being named to the Western Athletic Conference's All-Decade Team. In addition, a two-time Academic All-American, Hennings has been inducted into the GTE Academic All-American Hall of Fame as well as the College Football Hall of Fame.

His exemplary achievements put him at the top of many draft lists and earned him a spot on the Dallas Cowboys' roster, but Hennings postponed his entry into the National Football League to fulfill his commitment to the U.S. Air Force. He entered the

Euro-NATO program, a training program for top pilots, and soon found himself at the controls of the A-10 Thunderbolt.

During his four-year stint with the Air Force, Hennings flew forty-five missions in support of Operation Provide Comfort in northern Iraq, an effort that helped provide relief and humanitarian aid to Kurdish refugees. He received two aerial achievement medals, a humanitarian award, and an outstanding unit award for his actions in the service.

After his discharge, Hennings joined the Dallas Cowboys, quickly earning a starting position as a defensive lineman.

Today Chad is an author and the president of Hennings Management Corporation, a marketing and consulting company. As such he is a popular speaker to major corporations across the country. His other activities include speaking on values and motivation to numerous civic and nonprofit organizations as well as being a board member of Happy Hill Farm Academy. He is the founder of Wingmen Ministries, which works to show men, in a practical, nonthreatening way, how to grow closer to God and to live out their destiny in Christ, with other men supporting them. More information on Wingmen can be found at www.wingmendfw.com.